Cyber Safety for Everyone

By
JaagoTeens

FIRST EDITION 2017

Copyright © BPB Publications, INDIA

ISBN : 978-81-8655-152-8

LIMITS OF LIABILITY AND DISCLAIMER OF WARRANTY

Distributors:

BPB PUBLICATIONS
20, Ansari Road, Darya Ganj
New Delhi-110002
Ph: 23254990/23254991

BPB BOOK CENTRE
376 Old Lajpat Rai Market,
Delhi-110006
Ph: 23861747

COMPUTER BOOK CENTRE
12, Shrungar Shopping Centre,
M.G.Road, BENGALURU–560001
Ph: 25587923/25584641

DECCAN AGENCIES
4-3-329, Bank Street,
Hyderabad-500195
Ph: 24756967/24756400

MICRO MEDIA
Shop No. 5, Mahendra Chambers, 150
DN Rd. Next to Capital Cinema, V.T.
(C.S.T.) Station, MUMBAI-400 001
Ph: 22078296/22078297

Published by Manish Jain for BPB Publications, 20, Ansari Road, Darya Ganj, New Delhi-110002 and Printed him at Akash Press, New Delhi

Foreword

Children's online life is different from those of grown-ups, if their online safety is a constant worry this book is a great resource to use. It tells you the kind of trouble children can get into, when they are online, and suggests simple yet effective ways to deal with such situations.

JaagoTeens has written the book based on their live interactions with students, and most of the examples given here are true incidents. Schools have been inviting them for repeat sessions because they are aware of the issues plaguing students of various age groups, and are able to address the same.

This book is a must-read for every parent, teacher or child who wants to avoid the temptations and perils of cyberspace.

New Delhi

1st June, 2017

M Ejazuddin

Scientist 'F'

Ministry of Electronics and
Information Technology

(MEITY)

About the Authors

The authors - Leena Gurg and Usha Subramaniam - felt a dire need to promote internet safety. Thus, along with close friends, they formed JaagoTeens, a Registered Society, in April 2010.

Employing multiple formats, including highly vibrant and innovative game-based learning workshops and events,JaagoTeens have addressed over 80,000 people. Ably assisted by enthusiastic and trained college volunteers, the team encourages positive use of and responsible behaviour on the internet.

Online challenges and experiences collected during these workshops have been documented and some have been compiled into this extremely helpful book.

Leena (M.Sc.(Hons.) Physics, PG diploma in Computer Science and Applications, B.Ed.), a teacher for over 25 years, and Usha, a freelance writer, have put together their skills to write this unique and engaging book which is particularly relevant in this internet age.

Acknowledgement

We deeply acknowledge the valuable contributions of all our families, as also our members, including Sanjukta Sahni, Anita Rastogi and Naveen Gurg and, not to forget each and every college volunteer.

Without them all, this journey would not have been possible.

Table of Contents

Foreword .... *iii*

Table of Contents .... *vi*

Chapter 1. An Introduction to Internet Safety 1

Chapter 2. Real World and the Virtual World 5

Chapter 3. Basic Do's and Don'ts 15

Chapter 4. Protection of very young kids(5 to 8 year olds) 23

Chapter 5. Online Gaming 31

Chapter 6. Recognizing Cyberbullying and dealing with it 38

Chapter 7. Privacy of Personal Information 48

Chapter 8. Online Predators 61

Chapter 9. Smartphone Safety 79

Chapter 10. Safe Online Payments 87

Chapter 11. Laws that protect against Online Harassment 103

Chapter 12. Online Plagiarism 118

Chapter 13. Privacy Settings for Facebook, Instagram, SnapChat 124
            and other online platforms

Chapter 1. An Introduction to Internet Safety

If you belong to Gen X it is quite likely that you did not grow up with the internet. Do you feel troubled as you watch young children traverse this vast abyss of uncensored information, completely uninhibited, and without any adult supervision?

A lot of you, probably, also feel out of the loop and

- worry about where your children go online
- wonder if they will talk to you in case of any online trouble
- think of controlling their usage but stop short not wanting to block their use of the latest technology

This book can solve your dilemma, it tells you about the mistakes young users are likely to make and how these can be avoided or overcome. The book is meant for parents and teachers and also for every person who uses the internet, whether 8 or 80 years old. Each one will hopefully find some pertinent information in this book.

Online Safety Issues

In this book, we discuss the entire gamut of online safety issues, such as:

- Understanding that the internet is a very public space, with our online lives and real-world lives closely intertwined, each affecting the other.
- Importance of Netiquette, good etiquettes when online, and importance of leaving clean digital footprints
- Tips for protection of very young kids (5yr-8 yr), when online
- Cyber-bullying /online abuse: Staying away from online abuse and steps to deal with cyber abuse

Gen X are people born between the mid 1960's and the early 1980's.

Gen Y covers people born between the 1980's and the year 2000, they are also called the millennials.

- Identifying and keeping potential online predators and pedophiles at a distance
- Knowing what information is considered as personal information and why it is to be kept private
- Awareness of IT Act, including clauses that deal with hacking, impersonation, stealing of another's online data, cyberbullying, etc.
- Gaining knowledge of (post-Nirbhaya) women-centric laws to tackle online sexual harassment, voyeurism and stalking
- Concept of plagiarism and importance of avoiding plagiarism and copyright violation
- Learning how to modify privacy settings on FaceBook, Whatsapp, LinkedIn, Instagram, SnapChat, Twitter, Flickr, Pininterest, to ensure one's personal safety.

Reason for writing this book

We founded JaagoTeens, a society registered in April 2010 under the Societies Registration Act of 1860, and are committed to promote a responsible and safer internet ecosystem.

We have conducted close to 250 workshops and events in schools, colleges, NGOs, as well as institutions like National Bal Bhavan (every year), National Book Trust's World Book Fair, etc. reaching out to over 80,000+ children, parents and teachers.

A team of dedicated college volunteers assist us in conducting the workshops. Our volunteers benefit in a number of ways, the work gives them a chance to give back to the community, helps them learn public speaking skills and without doubt adds to their job resume.

We have been regularly compiling our experience at these events, and this includes what students said or asked. In this book, we have summarized a lot of what we learnt as we interacted with the students. We feel that this book can prove to be a useful resource for anyone who wishes to know about internet safety. It can be used to introduce

JaagoTeens is a registered society that works to promote a responsible and safer internet ecosystem.

Children don't think of consequences! 13% students said that they had uploaded photographs that they would not want to share with their family!

internet safety to students and to ensure that safety becomes second-nature to them.

Chapter Format

In each chapter of the book you will find a combination of the following elements.

True Incident/dilemma

Some chapters begin with a true incident/dilemma with the solution to it hidden somewhere in the chapter, for instance Ashmeet and Devang (names changed) were friends; Devang asked Ashmeet to send some nude pictures of hers, she refused but then very reluctantly sent him a picture. After some time, Devang shared this picture with his friends and it soon became public. How did Ashmeet deal with this difficult situation?

Practical Tips

A couple of "Practical Tips"; these are simple to-do points that one could implement right away to make the online journey safe and fun. For example, how to create strong passwords, how to deal with cyberbullying, how to keep information on your smartphone safe, how to lodge a complaint with the cyber police, etc.

Survey Results

A few results of surveys conducted by JaagoTeens, for instance*

- 13% students said that they had uploaded photographs that they would not share with their family! This revelation got us into action and we now urge students to take privacy of their photographs and other personal information very seriously. We also clarify to them that no privacy setting is fool proof and one needs to think that once something is posted online there is no guarantee that it will remain private as the internet is a very public space.

- 28% students were sure they could guess the age of a stranger with whom they were interacting online, another 64% yielded 'sometimes', thus laying bare the utter naivety of their tender adolescent minds!

- In a college survey, we asked students if they would talk to their parents/guardians about any uncomfortable online experiences.

Conversation starters for teachers and parents

Some suggestions for conversation starters for parents/guardians, some ideas on how to get talking to children about Internet Safety. For example, to tell a child about safe online gaming and to draw their attention to the age-rating mentioned on games, to tell children when and whom to report to in case they are faced with any disquieting situations.

---

* *Our findings are based on surveys conducted in private schools of New Delhi, India.*

Teaching ideas

You will find lots of teaching Ideas. These can be used by both, parents as well as teachers.

- **Simple craft ideas**, for instance making a double-sided mask to explain that a person pretending to be a handsome 15-year-old might actually be a 50-year-old abuser.

- **Scripts for puppet shows**, for example 'Three Red Flags' in Chapter 8 titled "Online Predators" can be used by children to do a puppet show/play and this can then be used to teach children to recognize signs of online abuse.

- **Ideas for games** that can be played in the classroom. For instance, our JaagoTeens, 'Be a Net Smartee' board game is extremely effective in communicating internet safety messages to young children.

Since teachers are always strapped for time, we've tried to make the teaching activities easily implementable. All of our activities are tried and tested and have been used successfully with hundreds of students.

Easy to Read

Discussion of all topics is kept simple with plenty of sub-headings for quick and easy reading.

> Let your child know who are the trusted adults they can go to in case of any online trouble

Chapter 2. Real World and the Virtual World

The following is a true incident reported to us by a college student:

Ashmeet (name changed) had a big-time crush on Devang (name changed). They became friends on FaceBook and were soon talking to each other every day. Ashmeet felt really close to Devang. One day, Devang pleaded with her to send him a nude photograph of hers. She refused him outright, but Devang continued to beg of her to send him just one pic. She finally relented and sent him a partially nude pic of hers.

But what happened next completely shattered Ashmeet. She came to know that Devang had circulated her nude pic among his friends. She started getting harassing calls and messages. They called her a sl**!! The picture just seemed to be everywhere, even people in the colony, where she lived, seemed to know about it.

This continued for weeks and months. Finally, she made up her mind to bring this to an end as she could no longer bear the humiliation being piled on to her.

She spoke about the incident to someone and this person helped her deal with the situation. Who do you think helped her out?

Find the answer to this question in this chapter.

Introduction

Do you use the internet? If you do, you are one of the estimated 3 billion people who go online, congratulations!

Roughly 46% of the world's population has access to the internet today, and interestingly, in 1995, just 1% of the world population was using the internet[1].

India has 462,124,989 internet users.

(Source: Internet Live Stats)

If people post something online, they need to know that any of those 3 billion people might see their post. One might think that this is something impossible, but let's take the example of the "Gangnam Style" video, it has been viewed, on YouTube, over 2.5 billion times.[2]

And this means that any other post can similarly go viral and be viewed by millions of people from all over the world.

Let us compare the number of people on the internet with those in the physical world. Any public place like a busy market or a railway station, or even the Kumbh mela (12 crore people attended it in 2013), has far fewer people than the internet. But even with such a large number of users here, the internet is deceptively quiet! This leads one to believe that one is all alone in the online space, but that is not true. One has to constantly keep reminding oneself that the internet is a public space where lots of other people are constantly reading and watching what other people are posting.

> Think of the maximum number of people some of your posts might have reached and now think of the maximum number of people these posts *could* have reached!

'Safety' in the Real World Extends to the Virtual World

The dictionary meaning of safety is to be in a state of being safe and protected from danger or harm. Extending the definition to the virtual world, a person needs safety or protection against online dangers, here too. Online dangers could be identity theft, harassment, malware and phishing attacks, access to inappropriate and obscene content, pedophiles, terrorists, etc. etc.

Why are So Many People Online?

The internet is a wide and varied place; with people using it in many different ways:

- A lot of communication in the form of emails, chat messages or **VoIP** is done over the internet. Social networking sites

[1] (http://www.internetlivestats.com/internet-users/)

[2] (https://en.wikipedia.org/wiki/List_of_most_viewed_YouTube_videos).

have made it easy for people to keep in touch with their friends and family.

- People are constantly looking up the internet for information, on jobs, health, the latest news, or some government services etc.

- Students find it useful to view online classes and working professionals are able to upgrade their skills through online courses.

- People bank online, shop online, book travel or movie tickets, saving a lot of time and effort in the process.

- Last but not the least, the internet is used for entertainment, some of its most popular forms being music and videos. A word of caution here, make sure that you understand the terms of use for all content you view and do not violate any copyright rules for media files that you may download. Check the terms of use and make sure you abide by them. This topic is covered in detail in Chapter 12 titled, 'Online Plagiarism'.

Are you feeling left out because you do not know how to use the internet. Nothing can replace your real-world experience, so just go ahead and hone your internet skills.

The internet has seeped into so many areas of our lives, leaving practically nothing untouched. Looking at the current trend one can only expect it to be more deeply entrenched in people's lives in the future, and whether we will greatly benefit from it or not, time alone will tell.

Real World and the Virtual World

Internet users are denizens of two worlds, the Real World and the Virtual World; sounds strange, but isn't it true? People exist on the Earth, the Real World, but when they go online, they move into the Internet world or the virtual world. Next, let us compare the behaviour of people when they are in these two different worlds. People who live in the real world are largely law-abiding citizens. They have learnt to conform to the rules and regulations of a structured and disciplined society.

Nevertheless, we know that not all people in the real world are law abiding, there does exist a segment that breaks the law, these could be small-time or big-time criminals, could be drunkards, robbers, abusers, murderers, rapists, smugglers, terrorists, fraudsters etc. Parents caution children against them, giving them simple safety tips, "don't take toffees from strangers..." "Return home before dark" ..."do not talk to unknown people" ...etc.

But what about the virtual world, do such people exist there? They do, and cybercrime does exist in the virtual world too. According to various newspaper reports the number of cybercrimes committed in India have been increasing each year. It may have touched a humungous figure of 3,00,000 in 2015, almost double the level of the previous year, an ASSOCHAM-Mahindra SSG study says[3].

Therefore, the same cautionary messages of the real world needs to go out to children in the virtual world. The messages might change to "never accept gifts from online friends" ..."do not chat with unknown people" ..."do not open links sent by unknown people," never go out alone to meet people whom you first meet online" ...

Can Parents' Guide Children on the Internet, just as they do in the Real World?

According to the Interpol website, *'Crimes against children are facilitated by the Internet, the increased use of which in recent years has led to a huge rise in offending.'* [6]

The present generation of parents, teachers and educators is not very internet-savvy, and often feel ill- equipped to guide youngsters when they are online. That might be true, but in a lot of difficult situations, it is not their internet knowledge, but it is their real-world life experience that comes in handy and helps them solve problems pertaining to the internet. After all, the offenders on the internet, are real people, and grown-ups are well-familiar with their antics.

For adults, getting familiar with the internet goes a long way in helping them keep their own children safe. A recent article in India Today [4] , says that the Delhi Police has seen an increasing number of offences on the internet where children are involved either as accused or as victims. They would like the involvement of parents, in addition to the school authorities, to work towards curbing such offences.

---

[3] *Details of this can be read at the following link.* http://www.assocham.org/ newsdetail.php?id=4821

[4] http://indiatoday.intoday.in/story/cyber-crimes-cops-to-rope-in-schools/1/ 578907.html

[6] http://www.interpol.int/Crime-areas/Crimes-against-children/Crimes-against-children

The article says that:

"Internet is easy to access. Inquisitive children soon know more about the Internet than the parents. Hence, it would be better if, as a parent, one gets involved in their Internet activities so that they can be taught to be safe".

Steps to Get One Get Started on the Internet

1. Switch on the computer/smartphone and make sure you are connected to the internet. Look for a web browser and double click to open it. Now, if you are online, you are using a **web browser**. Check your web browser. It is quite likely that it is Chrome, Internet Explorer, Safari or Firefox, if it something different it does not matter, all web browsers do the same thing, they let you access the internet.

2. If you know the address of a particular website type it into the address bar.

3. If you don't know any web address, just type in a topic that interests you, into the search box. A few options will be displayed on the screen. Choose one of these and click on it, a web page will open.

4. Move around on the webpage. Just observe how it looks, read the address bar, notice as you move the mouse around the pointer changes in some places, these are links.

5. If you click on one of these links, other web pages will open. A link is generally highlighted or is in a different colour so that you can locate it easily.

6. Repeat the above steps a couple of times, it can be quite an interesting experience.

7. Next, you could take help from someone to create an email id. Ask for someone's email id and send them an email.

8. Visit social networking sites and sign up on them. Add your friends and again spend some time exploring around. Remember to avoid posting personal information about your own self or your family.

9. Soon you will be zooming around happily exploring lots of new and interesting sites. *Give yourself time and don't be too hard on yourself if you are not able to understand things. Take help from a friend, your family or children. You can also look up some video tutorials on YouTube. These will give you step by step instructions on how to use the net. To find these videos, type 'Basics of Internet' or 'Internet for beginners', into the search box, and then choose from the various tutorials that show up.*

Answer to the Real-life Incident that We Narrated at the Beginning of the Chapter

Ashmeet was very close to her grandmother. She told her everything about the sexting incident.

Grandmother's first reaction, of course, was that of shock and anger. After she had calmed down, she was thinking really hard. After sometime, Ashmeet noticed granny call up Aunt Leela. She had a very long discussion with her. Aunt Leela was a family friend and she was a very well reputed advocate.

It was strange, but somehow Ashmeet felt greatly relieved after talking to granny. All along her greatest worry, had been- "What if granny gets to know of this?"

Her grandmother suggested Ashmeet have a conversation with Devang and inform him that

- *her family knows of the incident.*

- *he must immediately delete all copies of the photograph and must make sure he does not forward it to anybody else.*

- *grandmother will soon be talking to his parents and will be telling them about the incident.*

- *according to the recent amendments in the IPC, such behaviour is called voyeurism and it is a punishable offence. According to Section 354C, "Where the victim consents to the capture of the images or any act, but not to their dissemination to third persons and where such image or act is disseminated, such dissemination shall be considered an offence under section 354."*

Granny did not know how to use a computer but she certainly knew how to fight back people who were troubling her dear granddaughter. She used her real-life experience to help Ashmeet deal with the bullies.

The support of her grandmother provided Ashmeet tremendous confidence. It was not possible for her

Do you know your IP (Internet Protocol) address?

If you want to know your IP address type in 'what is my IP' in the Google search box and your IP address will be displayed.

to completely undo the damage that had been done, but her family's support had helped her tide over the crisis. Now everything was normal though still, at times, her classmates teased her. Her cousins still don't want to talk to her but that is okay, the worse is over for her.

Anonymity on the Internet is a Myth, an IP Address Identifies You Uniquely

In the real world, say you are talking to someone, you are aware of the physical presence of the person, there is no ambiguity regarding his/her identity.

But when you are online it is very difficult to establish the true identity of a person. You might think you are talking to 'Alia' but it might actually be 'Rohit'. If it very easy to get fooled because the cues for recognizing a person are not available online.

It is useful to know that the IP address can be used to trace a user, IP address is short for Internet Protocol address. It is a number that looks like this 59.178.223.189.

Shri M. Ejazuddin, Scientist 'F', Ministry of Electronics and Information Technology warns, "People indulging in illegal activity in the internet world might spoof their IP address so that they are not caught."

Several programs are also available online, where if you type in an IP address it will give you details about the ISP(Internet Service Provider) of that user, the country, city and approximate latitude and longitude from which that IP address is being used.

It is important to take one's online identity seriously. The feeling of anonymity might also create a mistaken perception that it is easy to hide one's identity but that is also not true. One needs to also ensure that one's computer resources is not used for any illegal or malicious activity because all misuse will be traced back to the owner of that resource.

Cyber police are incharge of stopping cybercrime.

Cybercrime is committed using a computer with an internet connection. It could be done to steal a person's identity or sell contraband or stalk victims or disrupt operations. Many times, malevolent programs are used for this purpose.

Police can Track an Offender

Police can take action against the offender if:

1. Someone by means of any communication device or computer resource cheats by personation. By Section 66D of the IT Amendment Act 2008, the punishment for this is Imprisonment of either description for a term which may extend to 3 years and the person is also liable to pay a fine which may extend to one lakh rupees.

2. If someone fraudulently or dishonestly makes use of the electronic signature, password or any other unique identification feature of any other person, this is known as identity theft and the person shall be punished with imprisonment of either description for a term which may extend to three years and shall also be liable to a fix fine which may extend to rupees one lakh. This is in accordance with Section 66C of the IT Amendment Act 2008.

JaagoTeens Survey

Our question to college students was, "Who is the best person to teach school children about Internet Safety?"

(A) Parents

(B) Teachers

(C) Friends

The following pie chart shows the distribution of the answers of male and female respondents.

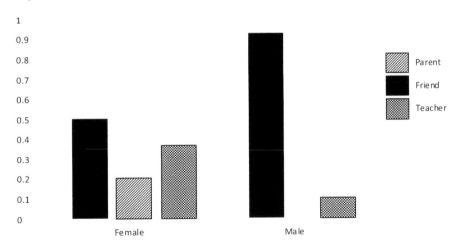

The response of 159 college students was recorded. This showed that about 52% of female respondents would like parents or teachers to talk to them, out of which 35% would prefer a teacher.

Surprisingly, amongst male respondents a mere 9% said they would have their teachers talk to them, with none of them wanting to discuss the topic with their parents, it was simply friends all the way for them!

To probe further, we conducted an online survey and given below are the answers of girls and boys, all in the age group of 18-20 years. Our question was *"Why is it that very few students are willing to talk to parents, is it because parents don't know how to use the internet?"*

Girls said:

1. Nowadays, most parents are familiar with the internet but most of them would rather talk to their peer group than to their parents.

2. Their peer group are not aware of the realities that exist in society. So, it to better to approach a parent or a trusted adult.

3. Parents can give you good advice if you share your stories with them, and this is despite the fact that they do not have online skills.

4. Parents don't even know how these sites operate then how you do expect them to be able to deal with situations that arise on them. So, all they do in such cases is completely cut-off their child's access to the internet, which is very unfair.

5. Another student had something interesting to say, she said, not all families are orthodox. Sometimes our own mind set is conservative and that stops us from sharing our stories with our parents.

Boys said:

1. A boy said that it gets a little uncomfortable to talk to parents. Most boys seemed to agree with this view and said that they don't like to discuss such topics with their parents.

No more explanations from boys, they had nothing else to add.

Hence the debate continued, with most of the responses coming in were from the girls. Do let us know what do you think is the reason for children to not share their online experiences with parents.

Teaching Activities

Activity 1: Real World and Virtual World

Objective: To compare the real world and the virtual world.

Material required: Paper, pencil, color pencils

Steps

1. Ask the students to draw two charts depicting the real world and the virtual world.

    The following picture can be used to help children visualize but let them use their own creativity to express any ideas that they might have.

    The white circle on the left is a representation of the real world and the dark segment indicates the 'bad people', the law breakers. The white circle inside the computer screen indicates the people who are on the internet. Once again the dark segment indicates the people who might indulge in malicious online activities.

2. Ask them to write 5 safety messages for the real world and then 5 safety messages for the virtual world.

Discussion Starters- for Parents/Guardians

1. Ask children if they like using the internet.
2. Ask them about the different things they do on the internet.
3. Ask them what is their favourite online activity.
4. Talk about what you do on the internet and tell them why you enjoy using the internet and what are the difficulties that you face.

Laugh and listen to whatever the children have to say. Take interest in what they are saying and try not to be judgmental. This is an opportunity for you to learn about what they do on the internet, you might be surprised to find that a child's use and understanding of this technology is very different from yours.

Chapter 3. Basic Do's and Don'ts

Simran (name changed), a young college student, belongs to a fairly conservative and orthodox family, she has been volunteering with us, at JaagoTeens, for more than a year. She has attended our training sessions, and has learnt the rules of safe net usage. She has also addressed her peer group on this issue. A Latin proverb "By teaching, we learn," perhaps derived from the Roman philosopher Seneca, she feels holds true for understanding internet safety.

Simran told us a few days back, "Somebody created a fake profile of mine and the person used my pictures for this. This is despite the fact that I am very careful when I am online, and I do not share my pictures with anyone other than my close friends."

How do you think Simran dealt with this matter? Find the answer to this question in this chapter.

Online Safety has rules that are easy to follow.

Introduction

Parents and educators do bring yourself up to speed with the internet and do not hesitate to take help from others to do that! It helps to be aware of your child's online habits and friends. *Recently during a school workshop in New Delhi, we asked the Class 5 students of a school at what time do they go to bed? The conversation started when a bright young kid said that at times he feels stressed out and he also has a headache when he is in school. Surprisingly, a fairly large number of other children likewise said that they too suffered from frequent headaches. We found that most of these 9 - 10-year-old students are sitting at their computers till close to midnight. Some confided to us: "till 12, even 12.30 at night, ma'am". This meant that the children were sleeping just for about six or six and a half hours and their internet usage was cutting into their sleep time. As the discussion continued, most of them said that their parents were not aware that they were online till late night.*

Do try to make Internet surfing a family pastime! There's plenty to explore out there. Spend some time with the children, see what sites they visit and simply have fun watching what they do. Ask them to teach you a couple of things about the internet. **Keep the lines of communication open with young** users in the family. Let them know whom to talk to in case of any online trouble. Educate them that each one is responsible for one's own safety; thus, the need for Net safety rules.

Here are a couple of Do's and Don'ts that we have gathered from our interaction with students.

Do's

IDs and Usernames:

Choose them carefully. They should not make you feel uncomfortable years later! For instance, while you are in primary school, your email id might have been "Hot_Chips95@gmail.com", but you certainly don't want to use that id when you are in college and definitely not when you are applying for a job, so either change your usernames and IDs as per your requirement or create them with more thought.

Personal Information

Do think carefully before revealing or sharing any personal information such as age, date of birth, marital status, relationship status, names of family members or financial information, when online. Your address, location, etc. must remain private. When you are downloading an app onto your smartphone, make sure you understand the permissions that you have granted to the app and the information that it can access on your phone. If you do not know what some permissions mean, go online type the word into the search engine and read up the information that shows up.

Report Mean or Uncomfortable Messages

If you find a message is sexual in nature or is meant to harass or threaten someone, you can contact your ISP(Internet Service Provider) for assistance. You should be able to find their contact details on your bill or on their website.

Do not reveal too much personal information, online.

It takes time to configure privacy settings so be patient and follow the instructions with patience.

Ask children to always inform you in case such messages are received. Don't forget to save evidence and do not hesitate to lodge a complaint with the cyber police in such situations.

Curb Excessive Use of the Internet

Keep the computer in a room frequented by family members. If you find your child is using the internet late in the night, curb this practice gently and patiently. Let the child be online only when other family members are awake, this makes it easier to keep a tab on their activities.

Privacy Settings

Make it a habit to configure the privacy settings when you create a new account. Many a times, the settings might be upgraded and the settings that you painstakingly configured may no longer be valid, so keep reviewing your privacy settings periodically.

Cyberbullying

Do caution children in strictest terms about the perils of cyberbullying and encourage them to share any awkward situations with you. Teach children netiquettes, the correct and acceptable way of using the internet. Urge them to treat others as they would have others treat them. This is also a good opportunity to teach them about gender equality. Ask them to treat girls and women with respect, when they are online.

Child-friendly Search Engines

Do install child-friendly Search Engines if you have young children at home! Their layout is definitely appealing to young children. Search the net for 'search engines for kids' and try them out.

Filtering Software

Do install filtering software. Children are highly impressionable and the internet is an Information Superhighway so make sure you know what kind of information they have access to!

Anti-virus Software

Do update and run your anti-virus software frequently. A computer virus is a small software program that spreads from one computer to another

Do not ignore cyber bullying. It can negatively impact one's health and well-being and should not be ignored.

Spend some time with your children when they are online. Get to know their favourite activities. It is amazing to watch them use this technology.

and interferes with computer operations. (Source: https://support.microsoft.com)

New viruses are continuously being released, so updating the anti-virus program will keep you protected against the latest malware. You always have the option to search for and download a free anti-virus program.

Browser

Do regularly upgrade your browser to its current version as the updates generally have important security warnings and protection features. For example, the latest versions of Safari and Internet Explorer warn you if you have navigated to a suspected phishing site so always update the software.

Passwords

Do keep different passwords for your social networking site and other sites, like your financial web pages, email accounts etc. Your password ideally should be a combination of numbers, small and capital letters, punctuation marks, and should be at least eight characters in length.

Don'ts

Do Not Share Passwords

Do not share your password with anyone, not even with your best friend. A password can allow access to your account which can leave you open to harassment and exploitation. Just as personal items like a handkerchief, or a towel, or a toothbrush are not shared with others, similarly a password should be viewed as an item meant only for personal use.

Make sure not to share passwords with anyone, not even with your best friends.

No Personal Information in Passwords

Do not use words found in the dictionary to create passwords and neither use your spouse's or children's name or date of birth. Do not use your pet's name, or any other personal information. They are too obvious and easy enough to guess.

Photographs of family

Never post photographs of your family or children on publicly accessible web sites or newsgroups. If you are in the habit of posting pics on social networking sites, then make sure you have configured your privacy settings appropriately. It is best not to post your children's pics online and completely refrain from using their pic as your profile pic on Whatsapp or any other application.

Not Your Real Name

Ask your child to use a pseudonym or a fake name, when online. They should not give out personal details like their full name (first name + surname) or their email id on forums etc.

Meeting Online Friends

Don't allow your child to meet with an online 'friend'. Tell them why it is risky to do so. Accompany him/ her if such a meeting has to take place at all.

Obscene Messages

Don't ever respond to messages that are offensive, obscene, threatening, harassing or uncomfortable in any way. Report the incident to the cyber police. You will have to save the messages as evidence to be able to lodge the complaint.

Links Received

Don't click links received in emails or on private messages. The links that are contained in e-mails, from unknown persons, might sound enticing and make you eager to open them, but they could lead you to sexually explicit or inappropriate web sites. The links could lead you to fake websites that can steal your personal information or your financial information. Clicking on such links can install malware on your system. So, the bottom line is do not be in a hurry to click on unknown links.

Online Acquaintances

Do not easily believe or trust people you meet online. One could claim to be a teenage girl but may in reality be a 54-year-old person!

Online Claims and Offers

Do not believe all online claims and offers. Investigate, examine or consider carefully before making online purchases, or before having someone visit your house. Be cautious and talk to a couple of people and patiently read through online reviews before sending even a very small amount of money.

"You have won a new iPhone", never ever click on such links!

Never enter your credit card information if you feel even slightly unsure. Check online reviews about the service or product, but do not rely on them fully as they can also be fake, at times.

Plug-ins

Shri M. Ejazuddin, Scientist 'F', Ministry of Electronics and Information Technology suggests caution while using plug-ins. He says, "Many sites require plug-ins. If you find abnormal pages, like links to pornographic websites etc. showing up, then revert back the plug in."

Some well-known browser plug-ins are Adobe Flash player, Quick Time player etc. which might be required to play video files.

Long Hours Online

Do not ignore excessive usage of the Net by any family member. This eats into time available for productive work, rest and sleep so discourage children from being constantly online.

.exe files

Do not run any ".exe" files on your computer unless you are sure that the files are from a legitimate source.

Signed into Important Accounts

Do not paste a URL or script into your browser while you are signed into other websites, like your social networking page, email account, banking page etc. Do not forget to 'Logout' or 'Sign-out' at the end of a session, whether from your email or social networking or financial transaction page. In case you leave your laptop or computer unattended somebody else can easily log into your account and operate on your behalf.

In case you forget to log out, some networking sites like FaceBook allow you to log out remotely. So, make sure you log out especially in case of a shared device.

Always make sure you secure your phone with a password to prevent any unauthorized access to your accounts.

Remember Password Option

Do not select the 'remember password' option if you are using a shared computer. Most browsers like Google Chrome, Safari, Opera and Internet Explorer allow you to choose private or incognito mode. This means the browser won't save the sites that you visit. Shri M. Ejazuddin, Scientist 'F', Ministry of Electronics and Information Technology also suggests, "clear browsing history when you finish a session."

One needs to know that even after clearing one's browsing history, your Internet Service Provider and the website administrator can still see your browsing history.

Here is the answer to the situation that was mentioned at the beginning of this chapter:

Simran said she reported the fake profile to the social networking site and they removed it, and she was greatly relieved.

You can see that Simran was confident that she could take action and did not have to put up with harassment and the accompanying anxiety that such a situation can cause. She has learned to take charge of her own safety.

Simran said "therefore awareness regarding internet safety is important as it helps you deal with such situations. I don't think I would have spoken to my friends or reported to the website if the same situation had arisen, prior to my joining JaagoTeens. You gave me the confidence to take action.

Thank you, JaagoTeens. You all are really doing a great job".

JaagoTeens survey

We asked students both before and after we spoke to them about internet safety, "Is the Internet safe?"

Survey results are summarized below.

Before the students attended the internet awareness programme

11-15 year olds

- 57 % said the internet is not safe
- 37 % said maybe it is safe
- 6 % said yes, it is safe

9-10 year olds

- 32 % said the internet is not safe
- 64 % said maybe it is safe
- 4 % said yes, it is safe

After the students attended a JaagoTeens internet safety awareness programme

11-15 year olds

- 80 % said the internet is not safe
- 19 % said maybe it is safe
- 1% said yes, it is safe

9-10 year olds

- 69 % said the internet is not safe
- 25 % said maybe it is safe
- 6 % said yes, it is safe

The above figures show that if children understand the threats present online, they will automatically be more cautious and refrain from indulging in risky online activities.

Activities for Teachers

Activity 1: Five dos' and don'ts

Objective: To draw their attention to online safety

Material required: Paper and pencil

Steps

1. Ask students to prepare of list of 5 dos' and 5 don'ts on the Internet.
2. Discuss the points that the students raise and have an informal discussion with them.

Activity 2: Oh, this stinks!

Objective: To be able to distinguish between right and wrong online actions

Material required: Paper and pencil, or a blackboard if done in the classroom, a fresh fruit or flower and a rotten fruit or a stale flower.

Steps

1. Prepare a list of about 20 do's and don'ts, this can be also be done as a group activity. Write them on the black board.
2. Then ask children to prepare chits with one item written on each chit.
3. Next put a fresh fruit/flowers/bread (anything that smells pleasant) at one corner of the table and a rotten fruit/stale flower/rotten vegetable (anything that smells bad) at the other corner of the table.
4. Call children one by one, ask them to pick up a chit, read it and then go and place it in front of the fresh fruit or the rotten fruit depending on whether it is a do or don't, respectively. Then, ask them to pick up the fruit/vegetable and smell it. This activity helps to create better recall as here they are linking correct action with good, or pleasant smell and wrong action with bad or unpleasant smell.

Conversation starters for Parents

1. Have a simple discussion on a couple of do's and don'ts.
2. A fun activity that can be done with young kids. Prepare a list of about 10 do's and don'ts. Write each item on a small chit of paper.

   - Next put a fresh fruit/flowers/bread (anything that smells pleasant) at one corner of a table and a rotten fruit/stale flower/ rotten vegetable (anything that smells bad) at the other corner of the table.

   - Ask your child to pick up a chit and go and place it in front of the fresh fruit or the rotten fruit depending on whether it is a do or don't, respectively. They have to pick up the fruit/ vegetable and smell it too.

   - This can be more fun if they have a few more friends/siblings doing this activity with them.

Chapter 4. Protection of Very Young Kids (5 to 8 Year Olds)

Here are a couple of questions that primary school children asked us during an Internet Safety workshop at their school.

1. *If someone asks us to give them information about our father or mother, should we give it to them?*

2. *Why shouldn't we put our pictures online?*

3. *Why shouldn't we copy things from Wikipedia?*

4. *Is it okay to keep the web camera on when we talk to people?*

You can see from these questions how naïve children are. By talking to them and answering their queries one can help them ward off risks and stay safe. We have answered the children's questions in this chapter, to know our answers, please read further.

Introduction

Your greatest worry when very young kids surf the net is that they might stray into inappropriate content. This possibility does exist given that the Internet has a lot of obscene, violent and pornographic content.

A child might stray into such websites by way of:

- Innocent or misdirected word searches

- Unsolicited e-mail

- Just plain curiosity

- Misleading URLs and stealth website (one that deliberately resembles a well-known or familiar website and cashes in on the legitimate website's popularity to draw in visitors). For example, whitehouse.gov is the official website of The White House in

Young children might be using the internet but their understanding is like that of a child, so it is important to tell them about safe internet usage.

Washington, D.C. but whitehouse.com has nothing to do with The White House.

Parental controls like filtering software or a child-friendly search engines help to block out adult content, violent content and hate speech, they can also be used to monitor a child's usage of a computer resource and they might also allow a parent to limit the time that the child spends online.

Parental Controls: To Block Inappropriate Content

Filtering Software

This helps in blocking out content that is not appropriate for a young kid. This filtering software also works to keep your child away from pornography, violence and hate speech and to control as well as monitor their usage of the computer.

Shri M. Ejazuddin, Scientist 'F', Ministry of Electronics and Information Technology, recommends," use a purchased version of Internet Safety software. Free software may be accompanied with malware."

Cyber Patrol

http://www.cyberpatrol.com/

With Cyber Patrol, it is possible to set time limits for internet usage as well as computer games, filter inappropriate sites, words and page contents under 14 different categories. It scores on ease of use and creates usage log for periodic review by, say, a parent. For a detailed review go to: http://internet-filter-review.toptenreviews.com/cyberpatrol-review.html.

Net Nanny

http://www.netnanny.com/

Sometimes rated a notch above Cyber Patrol, apart from the standard functions of parental controls, including usage reports which can be received anywhere in the world, a new feature is monitoring of social networking sites. For a detailed review go to: http://internet-filter-review.toptenreviews.com/netnanny-review.html.

K9webprotection

http://www1.k9webprotection.com/

Once again, k9webprotection is a free Internet filter that enables parents to block and manage unsolicited Web content such as pornography, violence and hate speech. It also blocks sites like MySpace.

SafeSearch by Google

SafeSearch acts to filter pornography and other offensive content. To turn on this option, go to your main Google Settings page and scroll down to SafeSearch Filtering options. If you have a problem finding it, type "SafeSearch "while you are signed into Google. Then check the box next to "Turn on SafeSearch". And, don't forget to hit 'Save', it is near the bottom of the page.

Child-friendly Search Engines

There's a host of options available. Type "Child-friendly search engine for kids", into Google and then choose a search engine that you think your child will like.

Listed below are just 5 well-known and popular children's search engines that omit adult content and sites from their searches. Most of the search engines have a colourful look that makes it interesting and fun for children to use.

You can either make this your home page or you can bookmark it so that your kid can use this browser to search for any information when they are online. The instructions for different browsers will be slightly different. You could explore one of these options or more options that are available online.

1. Yahoo! Kids (earlier known as Yahooligans) which is especially for age group 7 to 12 years.

2. www.safesearchkids.com (a search engine from Google where safe search is always on)

3. www.askkids.com (from the Ask Jeeves stable).

4. www.KidsClick.org: a web search for kids by librarians neatly lists reference topics under 15 broad categories.

5. www.dibdabdoo.com

6. www.factmonster.com

To block pop-ups in Google Chrome, Internet Explorer, Safari and Mozilla Firefox

Pop-ups are the windows that appear without your permission. To stop those pesky pop-ups from displaying in your web browser you need to configure the pop-up blocker. If you find that you are not able to stop the pop-ups or control them despite having configured the pop-up blocker, or if your home page has changed, then it is quite likely that your computer has malware on it. In such a situation take the following steps.

Whether you wish to enable or disable the pop-up blocker, the choice is yours.

1. Install an anti-virus program on to your system,

    you could consider downloading a free antivirus from the internet. Shri M. Ejazuddin, Scientist 'F', Ministry of Electronics and Information Technology says, "National Informatics Centre (NIC) and The Indian Computer Emergency Response Team (CERT-In) distribute anti-virus free of charge."

2. Thereafter, make sure you update it regularly as this alone can protect you against the latest threats.

The settings for a pop-up blocker are browser specific, follow the instructions below in case yours is Google Chrome, or Internet Explorer or Safari or Mozilla Firefox.

Shri M. Ejazuddin says, "Some plug-ins overwrite the pop-up blocker. The plug-in can be reverted if one notices such a compromise."

Google Chrome

1. Open Chrome.
2. At the top right, click More (the 3 vertical dots).
3. Click Settings.
4. Scroll down to the bottom of the page, now click 'Show advanced settings'.
5. Under "Privacy," click Content settings.
6. Scroll down till you find "Pop-ups". Select the option: 'Do not allow any site to show pop-ups (recommended)'.

Internet Explorer

1. Open Internet Explorer. Click the three horizontal dots.
2. Next, find Settings and click on it.
3. Click view advanced settings.
4. Find Block pop-ups and turn it to 'on'.

Safari

1. Choose Safari > Preferences, then click Security.
2. Select "Block pop-up windows," then deselect Allow WebGL and Allow Plug-ins.

Mozilla Firefox

1. Click the menu button ≡ and choose Options.
2. Select the Content panel.
3. In the Content panel configure settings for Pop-ups as per your choice.

Answers to Questions Given at the Beginning of the Chapter

1. *If someone asks us to give them information about our father or mother, should we give it to them?*

   Never give out any information about yourself or your family. Stop any further conversation with the person, and let your parents or a trusted adult know about this.

2. *Why shouldn't we put our pictures online?*

   If your picture is online it makes it easy for strangers to identify you, thus it is important to check with your parents or a trusted adult before sharing any pictures online. Make *sure you are only sharing the kind of pictures that you would not hesitate to share with your family. Also, make sure you are only sharing with people whom you know in the real world, and not with people whom you have first met online.* Shri M. Ejazuddin, Scientist 'F', Ministry of Electronics and Information Technology would like to caution children and tell them that,"Photos can be copied, morphed or re-posted. Hence pictures should not be posted casually'.

3. *Why shouldn't we copy things from Wikipedia?*

   - *Read the Wikipedia, understand what you read, then write the relevant information in your own words.*

   - *Do not try to mislead the reader into believing that what you have written is your own creation, if it is not. But one also needs to know that anyone in the world can edit Wikipedia. So, it might not essentially be a very authentic source of information.*

   - *By simply copying and pasting information you end up losing your*

Sit with the child and help him/her identify at least two trusted adults, people with whom he/she can share any uncomfortable online experiences.

own creativity and originality. To develop these skills, it is best to avoid copying and pasting information from online resources.

4. *Is it okay to keep the web camera on when I am talking to people?*

    A web camera should only be used in a parent's presence, it should not be used without adult supervision. There also exists a possibility of a hacker being able to control a web camera remotely, which means it might be turned on or off without your getting to know, so it is better to either disconnect it or cover it with a tape, when not in use.

Age Requirement for Email Accounts

Gmail says that the permissible age to create an email account is 13 years. If a child is under 13 years of age, and needs access to an email account, then a grown-up can let them use their account. Just make sure this account is separate from the one used for regular correspondence.

And a reminder for your email accounts, never click on links received from unknown people. They may contain malicious code that can contaminate your computer or may lead you to phishing sites.

Also, warn children to neither click nor call numbers that they might see if they happen to click on unknown links.

You can create an Apple ID for children under 13 years of age. These IDs allow them to participate in Family Sharing and use other Apple services such as iCloud, iMessage, FaceTime, and Game Center.

Buying Something Online

In real life, a trusted adult monitors purchases made by a child. In the same way, one needs to monitor online purchases that a child makes. This is necessary as a child

- might not be able to detect a spoof or a phishing website,

Monitor online purchases just as you control and monitor purchases that a child makes in real life.

- might get lured to make a purchase that a parent/guardian might not approve of
- might not report loss of money for fear of being rebuked.

So, it is preferable that grown-ups monitor all online financial transactions and make sure that no transactions are being done without their knowledge.

Let a child know whom to report to if he/she faces an uncomfortable situation, online

In this chapter, we discussed a few parental controls that can be used to monitor a child's online activities. However, one cannot underscore the importance of a simple conversation because any amount of technology based parental controls cannot replace a trusted adult's timely intervention. In the real world, in normal circumstances, a child lives in a space, be it the house, or park, or school that is monitored by caregivers. However online, children, knowingly or unknowingly, might step into places(websites) that can have abusive people in them. It is not possible for their trusted adults to supervise these online spaces. So, children need to know that they must talk to a trusted adult if they come across anything that makes them feel uneasy or unhappy.

At times, a parent might not understand a child's dilemma because they might not be very familiar with the internet. However, if a child has a few adults whom they can go to it is more likely that their complaint will be heard and given the attention it deserves.

Teaching Activities

Activity 1: Mud and Water

Objective: You cannot get back what you post once!

The internet is like a huge public notice board and once you have posted something here, there is no way of guaranteeing that someone, somewhere might not have seen it. Hence, it is very important to '*Think Before You Post*' things on the internet.

Materials required

A glass of clean water

Some mud, a teaspoonful

Yes, that's all. This is a very simple yet effective activity that can be done without any prior preparation.

Steps

1. Take the glass of water and take a sip from it. Next add some mud and exclaim – Oh, no! I want to drink this water. What do I do now?
2. Students will suggest that you can clean the water, they might suggest you use sedimentation, decantation, filtration etc.
3. Finally, they'll tell you,"go and throw the water, there is nothing you can do about it."

4. At this point ask them, "making the water drinkable again, is very, very tough!"

5. "Does something like this happen on the internet". Probe them a little further if you do not get satisfactory responses, "If you post something and…". It is quite likely that they are thinking now and you will start getting a lot of answers.

6. Then tell them

    ● Once you put in the mud (your post) you cannot control which part of the glass it spreads to.

    ● Besides cleaning up the water (removing the post) is next to impossible.

7. Some of them might say that undoing things online is very simple. Simply delete the post and it is gone. Tell them that someone might have already seen the post and copied it elsewhere. Explain to them that once you post something online, you might delete it at one place but you never delete it completely from the internet.

To explain this in greater detail to children who understand computer science, Shri M. Ezajuddin, Scientist 'F', Ministry of Electronics and Information Technology, adds, "deleting sends back an acknowledgement that a target has been found."

Conversation Starters for Parents

1. Encourage children to always report uncomfortable situations to a trusted adult, ask them not to keep unpleasant experiences to themselves.

2. Tell them that it is very difficult for children to gauge people's intention, especially when they are online. Ask them would they let a younger sibling work on the internet without any supervision. They would most likely say 'no', so tell them similarly they also need help and support from someone older to them.

3. Have a free and fair discussion with the child and see how can you best address a situation that might have necessitated the need to impose a blanket ban on a child's internet usage. It is quite likely that you felt your child could get into serious trouble if they continued to use the net. A ban might not work because there are a number of places from which a child might access the internet. So it is more important to explain to them why was the ban necessary and help the child avoid making the same mistake in future.

Chapter 5. Online Gaming

During a JaagoTeens workshop at one of the leading schools of Delhi, a 10 year- old student said:

I am addicted to the internet. I use it 4 hours daily but, I do nothing very constructive, I just keep playing games and watching videos. After your session, I realize this is wrong but how do I get over my addiction?

You can find JaagoTeen's answer to this question in this chapter.

Introduction

According to a JaagoTeens survey in 2014, in two leading schools of New Delhi, about 45% students play online games, with 54% boys and 34% girls spending time on online gaming.

As per another survey, playing online games ranked 4th amongst student's favourite online activities. They ranked their activities as follows:

1. interacting on social media,
2. downloading music and videos
3. searching for information
4. Playing online games

Games at the fourth place might not be fully correct, because a lot of them had ranked social media at the top of their list of activities but were actually using this as a platform to play online games.

During the course of our workshops in schools we get a lot of questions from students. Given below are seven commonly asked questions, each followed by what we answered.

1. **If I have been chatting with someone for a long time, why should I treat that person like a stranger?**

    JaagoTeens answer: Children might interact with unknown people on gaming sites, chat rooms or social media platforms. If they are talking to or interacting with the same person over an extended period of time, let's say 6 months or a year, they tend to lower their guard and start thinking of the person as a friend. So, it is important to remind them that any person whom they *first* meet online is to be always regarded as a stranger. The same caution that one would normally exercise with unknown people in the real world, needs to be maintained all throughout one's interaction with such people.

2. **I use a FaceBook account only to play online games, but I am not yet 13 years old, is it okay for me to be on Facebook?**

   JaagoTeens answer: We often find that students in the age group of 9-11 years, despite being underage, have accounts on FaceBook, and they say that this account is used only to play online games. For online gaming purposes, we suggest, children use gaming websites that cater to their age group, and when they are 13 years old, they join FaceBook.If a child is less than 13 years old then, according to the FaceBook Help Centre, he/she is not allowed to create an account on FaceBook. Children who are more than 13 years old, need to enter their age correctly and not give a false age, we tell students, "don't say you are 21 if you are 12 years old." For children 13-17y, FaceBook has some safety features, sensitive information like contact information, name of school, birthday will not be visible to a public audience. Their accounts cannot be found by search engines, however, this is not always true.

3. **What kind of username should I use on gaming sites?**

   A safe username is one that does not reveal your personal information. It does not have your name, age, gender, date of birth, location etc in it. For example, it is better to use 'k113' rather than 'hot_dude14', or 'cutiepie13', or 'manufan7', as a username.

   Avoid using the name of a celebrity, whom you admire, and also don't use your personal interests or hobbies while creating a screen name. For instance, if you are fond of a particular sport, let's say, cricket or football, then don't use information related to that sport in your screen name. The trick is to be able to think and invent a screen name that does not give out any personal information about you.

   Discuss your screen name with an older sibling or a trusted adult in the family, they might be able to help you out. To test your screen name ask them what information can they gather from your screenname.

4. **How can we hide our personal information on gaming sites?**

   JaagoTeens answer: Wherever possible, sign in as a guest user. In this way, you will be disclosing minimum personal information at the website.

   We suggest you use
   - An email id that you have created only for gaming and such purposes
   - Avoid putting your own name as a user name, use a pseudo name.
   - Avoid using usernames with words that make direct or indirect reference to sex and gender.

- Do not disclose your age, gender and location through your username.

5. **Why do we get <u>banned</u> from some gaming websites when we enter our correct age?**

JaagoTeens answer: All games have an age rating on them. If a user is under-age, and does not fulfil the age requirement of the gaming site, then his/her access to a game is blocked, and this is done to keep underage gamers away.

Most parents are not aware of the existence of an age rating on games so they might not check it before buying/downloading a game for their child.

For young children using Apple's Game Centre, one can disable multiplayer games (more than one person can play at the same time), adding friends and screen recording. To find out how to do this type "apple game center disable multiplayer, adding friends, screen recording" and follow the instructions that are displayed on the screen.

Games on Google play store are classified in accordance with IARC system (International Age Rating Coalition). Some places, like The Firefox Marketplace, Nintendo eShop, Windows Store have the game ratings displayed on their apps and games.

The age-rating standards given below will you give an idea on what basis is the classification done. This information is from the Google support page and can be found under the heading, "Rating Standards by country or region"/ "Other Countries" [7].

Rating	
3+	**Rated for 3+** Suitable for all age groups. Some violence in a comical or fantasy context is acceptable. Bad language is not permitted.
7+	**Rated for 7+** **May contain some scenes or sounds that are frightening for children. Mild violence (implied or non-realistic) is permitted.**
12+	**Rated for 12+** Violence involving fantasy characters and/or non-graphic violence involving human-looking characters or animals is permitted. Non-graphic nudity, mild language and simulated gambling are also permitted, but sexual expletives are not.

[7] *https://support.google.com/googleplay/answer/6209544?hl=en-IN.*

16+	**Rated for 16+** Realistic violence, sexual activity, strong language, use of tobacco and drugs, and the depiction of criminal activities are permitted.
18+	**Rated for 18+** Graphic violence, including depictions lacking motive and/or directed towards defenseless characters, and sexual violence are permitted. May also include graphic sexual content, discriminatory acts and/or the glamorization of illegal drug use.

6. **What is wrong with <u>games that are not meant for my age?</u>**

   Most video games have very elaborate graphics, and they might have content that is not appropriate for children below a certain age.

   The content might portray sexuality, violence, fear, horror, alcohol, tobacco, drug, crime, anti-societal activities, gambling, and parents might not want their under-age children to view such content.

   Hence, it is important for parents/trusted adults to read the description of the game before buying or downloading a game for their child.

10 practical tips from JaagoTeens College Volunteers for young gamers:

1. Before you download a game, check online reviews. Don't simply rush to download a game without checking what other people have said about the game. Also, make sure you only download games from reputed websites, else you run the risk of downloading viruses onto your computer.

2. Your username and password should not give out your personal information. Use something that is completely unrelated to your personal information.

3. Do not use your real name, and avoid using names that have suggestive words in them.

4. Create an alternate email id, don't use your personal email id while signing up for games.

5. Avoid signing in through your FaceBook account to play online games.

6. If you wish to play the higher levels where you need to make a payment, then check how secure and well known the gaming site is. Check its credibility, go through reviews and also do a thorough online search before you proceed to make a payment at the site.

7. Avoid talking to strangers in multiplayer games,.

8. Don't buy pirated games, and buy gaming consoles only from authorized retail outlets.

9. Make sure you have a good antivirus installed and that your machine is free from malware, spyware etc. Also make sure your operating system and web browser are updated.

10. Do not forget to sign out of your gaming account once you have finished playing.

Answer to question at the beginning of chapter- how to get over internet addiction

This was the question that we had posed at the beginning of this chapter.

A 10-year old's recent admission: I am addicted to the internet using it 4 hours daily to play games and watch videos, but doing nothing constructive. After your session, I realize this is wrong, but how do I get over my internet addiction?

A parent/ care-giver needs to work with the child to help him/her overcome such addiction. A blanket ban might prove to be counterproductive, so we suggest the following steps to help a child get rid of the habit of spending long hours online.

1. If a child does not get adequate sleep, it is quite likely that he/she will not be fully attentive at school, the next day. Hence, it is important to monitor a child's bedtime, serving them dinner etc on time, this helps keep their bed time fairly constant.

2. It is important not to allow electronic devices into a child's bed room. This curbs their temptation to play games, send messages and talk till late in the night. Make sure you know all the different devices that they might use to access the internet from, and also ensure that all these devices are outside their bed room, at night.

3. Parents need to ensure that their child is playing games that are meant for their age. It is not a good idea to let them play games that are meant for adults as that can negatively impact their psyche.

4. It is best to talk to the child and decide how much time and at what time the child can play online games. This will assist in limiting the time spent online. One has to also make sure that the child follows the schedule that has been mutually agreed upon.

5. Try and ensure that children are also playing outdoor games. Playing outdoors helps to ensure that they are tired enough to drop off to sleep which in turn reduces their temptation to stay awake and play online games. If you find that your child sleeps long hours in the afternoon because he/she is sleeping late at night, help the child modify his routine. Reduce the afternoon nap time so that they are not awake till late at night.

Parents, if your children wish to buy online games

It is preferable not to allow a child to make money-transactions on their own. If they end up buying goods for more than what you want them to, there is no way in which you can get your hard-earned money back. So, the best thing to do is to monitor all online purchases that a child makes.

The basic precautions regarding safe online payments can be found in chapter 10 titled, "Safe Online Payments".

Teaching Activities

Activity 1- Help Karamchand Jasoos allot safe screen names/ usernames to his team-members

Objective: Creating Safe User Names or Screen Names

Material required: Paper and pen

1. Divide children into two or more teams, try to have not more than 5 children in each group.

2. Ask them to think of a screen name. Next, ask them if the screen name reveals their name, age, gender, date of birth, country. If it does, ask them to think of a different name. The screen name should not have any indecent words in it.

3. Ask them to write the screen name on a piece of paper and then take up each screen name for discussion, check if it satisfies the criteria mentioned in point 2, given above.

4. Declare the team with the safest usernames as the winning team.

5. A few suggestions for safe screen names are

    - K113,

    - Corange5252,

    - gruganeel (anagram of my name "Leena Gurg", this is easy for me to remember and it does not give out my real name, you couldn't have guessed I used my name, until I disclosed it to you?)

6. Explain to children that a screen name like cutiepie13 or Angel40 could invite unwanted attention from abusers/pedophiles. So, it is a good practice to not ignore screen names, both while creating and when talking to other people.

Conversation Starters for Parents

1. Ask your child to name their favourite online games. If possible, try out these games yourselves, so you are aware of the kind of games they are playing.

2. Discuss the issue of age-rating with your child, they like to participate in such discussions but it is quite likely that they try and convince you that these age ratings are meaningless. See how best you can explain the need to respect age-appropriateness of content that they view.

3. One needs to keep reminding children to follow good netiquettes on gaming sites. Just because they are losing a game or are angry with an opponent, or they don't like an opponent, they cannot behave badly. Similarly, if someone is behaving badly with them they need to report to the gaming website and to you.

Chapter 6. Recognizing Cyberbullying and Dealing with It

This is a true incident that a college volunteer related to us, this happened when she was studying in Class 10:

Shreya (name changed) was interested in fashion designing and she posted pictures as well as sketches of some clothes that she had designed. Next day, many of her close friends called to tell her that someone had left highly derogatory remarks on her designs. Soon the post went viral and anonymous people made blatant suggestions, they said that she should be punished and some even said that she should be killed.!

Seated at her computer, Shreya wept silently. She finally decided to tell her parents. With tears rolling down her cheeks, she told them what had happened. Her father was furious and decided to take action.

One of her cousins helped them and they got to know that the remarks were not posted by multiple people, it was just one person who had posted all the comments under different names.

They also got to know that the perpetrator was one of Sneha's classmates. They were in for a rude shock when they came to know that the bully was the son of a close family friend of theirs.

Sneha's father contacted the boy's family and demanded that the posts be taken down. He was surprised when they failed to acknowledge the gravity of the situation, and did not ask their son to remove the rude comments. What do you think happened next? Read further to find out how this situation was resolved.

What is Cyberbullying?

First of all, let us take a look at the dictionary meaning of the words 'cyber' and 'bully'. Cyber

A victim of cyberbullying might not report bullying fearing that it might get worse if he/she reports it. But, this is not correct.

means related to or on the internet, and bully refers to a person who is uncultured, aggressive, rude, or a noisy troublemaker. So, when a bully operates in the realm of the internet, and troubles someone online, that behaviour is termed as cyber bullying.

The intention of the bully is to harass, annoy, intimidate, embarrass, ridicule or humiliate the victim by posting mean, derogatory or abusive messages.

Posting others Personal Information is also Cyberbullying

Did you know that disclosing personal information about others, comes under the ambit of cyberbullying? It is always an individual's choice as to what he/she wishes to post online, so posting information about others, without their permission, is tantamount to bullying the person.

Do not post a friend's picture without explicitly asking them if they are okay with your posting the pic. Also, mention to them where exactly do you plan to post the picture and send them a link so that they can view the information.

Do Complete Strangers Bully, Perhaps, 'No'?

During one of our JaagoTeens Teacher's workshops, one of the teachers related an incident of cyberbullying. She said that a young widow, who lived in her neighbourhood, was receiving harassing messages for a long time. They had assumed that the messages were being sent by some unknown person, a complete stranger.

Our JaagoTeens team told her that it is quite likely that the bully was someone known to her, and not a complete stranger. She was quite surprised at our guess and said that was true. When the police investigated the case, they found that a youngster living in the same building, and known to the lady, was indeed the culprit.

The teacher was inquisitive to know how did we guess that the perpetrator could be a person known to the victim. We told her that we have noticed in most incidents that students have shared with us,

If one is being bullied one needs to keep in mind that it is not the victim's fault, and it is necessary to report the bullying to stop it.

the bully is often someone known to the victim, and hence we made that guess in her case too.

The bully might know the victim in real life or might have gained familiarity with the victim by reading content written by the victim, maybe on a blog or a forum or a social website or while playing games at online gaming sites or through exchange of messages in a chat room.

Hence, it is very important that one is cautious while posting content and also while interacting with unknown people on gaming sites, chat rooms, and on social platforms.

To Stop a Cyberbully

The following are a few suggestions or steps that a victim might want to take to stop the bullying.

- First and foremost, try and **ignore** the comment. Cut off communication with the bully. Make sure that they are not able to contact you further. It is not your fault and *don't let the feeling that you might be hurting the bully overwhelm you. Nobody has a right to be mean and hurtful and you don't have to tolerate such behavior. Be kind to your ownself and work to put a stop to the bullying.*

- If the problem seems to persist or if you continue to feel unhappy or uncomfortable you **must** talk to a trusted adult/higher authority. Talk to someone who takes your side and understands how you feel. At times, the victim keeps quiet and doesn't tell others because they think that reporting the incident will only aggravate the problem. On the contrary, not dealing with a bullying incident only worsens the situation for the victim.

- If a bully knows that you are talking to others and taking help, they tend to improve their behavior because they are afraid of being punished for their bad conduct. It is good to let a bully know that you have reported their behavior to others and you have people who will stand up for you.

To deal with bullying one needs to get support from one's well-wishers. Without action, it is very unlikely for the bullying to stop.

- *The longer the bullying persists, the greater the harm it causes, and the more difficult it becomes to stop it.*
- It is important for children to discuss any bullying incident with a trusted adult so that their care-givers are able to decide if it can be dealt with at their level or the matter needs to be reported to the cyber police.

As per our JaagoTeens survey, the number of people sharing a bullying incident with others, is extremely small. Only 12% of 10-15 year old's whom we surveyed, said they had spoken to a trusted adult about a bullying incident.

Possible Reasons for Someone to Exhibit Bullying Behavior

1. It could be a feeling of superiority, the bully thinks that his/her victim belongs to a race, caste, creed or country that is inferior to the victim.
2. The bully might be looking for some material gain. By intimidating or threatening others he/she might be looking to get some direct or indirect financial gain.
3. it might be to control or manipulate others. The bully probably has a strong urge to have full control over people and situations. Such people are not able to let go!

Breaking Bullying Behaviour

Here we have discussed ways to handle a bully and this is based on our work at JaagoTeens.

If the bully realizes that his behavior can harm his self- interest it is quite likely that he will discontinue the bullying behaviour.

Bullies are generally devoid of empathy, which means they are not able to understand other people's feelings, so rationalizing or telling them that they are hurting others generally does not prompt them to stop. Therefore, if a child is a bully one has to help him develop empathy and make him understand that he is hurting others and he has no right to do so. It is important to work on this aspect so that the bully has a healthy relationships with other people when he grows up.

A bystander is a nonparticipant or uninvolved spectator.

Empathy is understanding and entering into another's feeling.

As a parent/teacher you could try the following steps to curb bullying behavior:

- Talk to a bully about some specific incidents where his behavior was improper. Tell the bully that such behaviour is not acceptable and warn him/her not to repeat it in future. He will have a lot of raving/ranting/tears but persist that the bullying should not happen again.

- Bullies feel that they are successful in controlling and manipulating their victims but don't like the fact that they can be punished for their poor conduct. So, let them know that you are collecting and saving evidence against them and you could be soon reporting them to a higher authority or to the cyber police.

- Explain to a bully that in the long run, his behavior will do him more harm than good. Tell him that gradually his friends will try and distance themselves from him and soon he will find himself completely isolated, as people will avoid his company. Also remind him that his friends might be joining him in the bullying, but this might be just to save themselves from being targeted by him.

- Tell the bully to mend his ways and works towards modifying his behavior.

The above are our suggestions on how to deal with a bully but if these don't work in your case, you might have to adopt a different strategy. But don't hesitate to take help from others, could be your peer group or it could be people in authority, maybe even a legal authority. Talking to others and seeking help is important while dealing with a bully.

One needs to also realize that there is no 'one fits all' solution for bullying instances so it always helps to talk to as many people as one can and not to hesitate in taking help from others.

How to Lodge a Police Complaint?

Let us first look at an answer to the incident that we discussed at the beginning of this chapter.

Shreya was interested in fashion designing and she posted pictures as well as sketches of some clothes that she had designed. Next day, someone had left highly derogatory remarks against her post. Soon the post went viral and anonymous people made blatant suggestions, they said that she should be punished and some even said that she should be killed.!

She finally decided to tell her parents. Her father was furious and decided to take action. The perpetrator was one of Sneha's classmates, and they were in for a rude shock when they got to know that the bully was the son of a close family friend of theirs. Sneha's father contacted the family and demanded that the posts be taken down. He was surprised when they did not ask their son to take down the rude comments.

Shreya's father decided to take legal action and contacted the police. The police intervened, the post was taken down and a formal apology was written by the perpetrator to the victim.

Now when Shreya looks back and thinks of the incident she feels that the best thing she did was to talk, she is glad she shared the incident with her close friends and her family. She is, of course, thankful to the cyber police for having taking action against the bully.

At times, if the bullying takes a serious turn, one might need to make a police complaint. To be able to lodge a complaint it is necessary for one to collect evidence, without evidence even the police cannot take action against a culprit.

Save up all emails, chats, posts, messages. Preferably take a screen shot (the next paragraph explains how to take one). A screenshot is a copy of the display on your computer screen. Make sure you also capture the bottom task bar that shows the date and time on your computer. Simply copying and pasting messages from posts is not the correct way to save evidence, as it is very easy to alter such text messages. However, editing a screen shot is not as simple so it is a better form of proof than a text message.

Taking a screen shot on a computer:

1. Press the key labelled "PrntScr" on your keyboard.

   When you press this key the image gets stored in the computer's memory so unless you paste it into a file it does not get saved on your computer.

2. Open Paint or a blank Word document.

3. Press Ctrl+V to paste the screenshot, also called a screendump.

4. Give the document a name and save it.

5. An alternate method is to press Windows and PrntScr, together

6. Then repeat the steps from point 2 onwards.

Taking a screen shot on a phone will be different. This varies from one model to another. To find how to take a screen shot type, "how to take screen shot + 'make and model of your phone'" and follow the instructions that show up.

You need a print out of the screen shot. To do that either transfer the screen shot from your camera to a device like a laptop/computer that can be connected to a printer. First, locate the screenshot on your phone. Next select and share it. You can email it to yourself or to an email account that you wish to use for the print out. Open the email account and take a print out of the screenshot that is attached in the email.

If you have an option of directly printing it from the phone, there is no need to email it.

An Example of a Situation Where People don't Remain Bystanders but Take Positive Action

I have noticed that, many a times, people don't remain silent spectators if they come across any bullying behaviour, online. They counter the bullying remarks, and this helps check the bully and dissuades others from joining in.

For instance, someone posted this comment on a YouTube channel, "Actually my question is immediately going to be, how the hell am i going to stop laughing at her (Indian) accent long enough for me to pay attention to this?"

This comment had 7 likes, which meant that some people had provided support to the bully.

A few weeks later, another YouTuber posted, "thank you so much for the lesson. I understood every single word clearly ..and plz don't pay attention to those trying to make negative comments. Best of luck :)".

Now don't you think the second user played a very positive role, he did not remain a silent observer, he behaved like a responsible netizen and most importantly, stood up against the bully.

Teaching Activities

Activity 1: Puppet Show

Objective: A puppet show that teaches children how to fight bullying (5y – 10y)

The puppet show has 3 characters. Rohan (boy), Anna (girl) and Sneezy (dog).

The following material will be required to make the three sock puppets that are used in this simple yet effective skit.

Material Required to make the Puppets

- 3 old socks
- 6 buttons for the eyes + 1 large button for Sneezy's nose + 2 small buttons for Rohan and Anna's nose
- Strands of black wool or golden wool for Rohan and Anna's hair.
- Felt pen or a marker pen or some black paint to draw the puppet faces
- Gum to paste the buttons on the socks
- 3 Placards

Making the Puppets

1. Wear the sock on your hand and move your thumb so you know where the mouth of the puppet will be. Draw the mouth. Next draw the eyes and nose.

2. Take off the sock and stick the button for the eyes and nose. Let the children color and decorate their puppets. **Do send us pictures of your puppets and puppet show, we would love to see them.**

3. Write 'Ignore', 'Stop' and 'Report', in caps, on each of the 3 placards.

Anti-Bullying Script for Puppet Show

Dialogues	Description of the scene
Boy- Rohan Girl- Anna Dog- Sneezy	Hold up a laptop on the side so that it seems that Rohan is working on the computer. Sound of his phone ringing. He does not notice.
Anna- "Rohan, I have been calling you, why didn't you pick up the phone. I was worried."	Anna comes in with Sneezy
Sneezy- Achoo Achoo.	Sneezy moves very close to Rohan
Rohan-"Hi Anna, Hi Sneezing Sneezy"- a little sadly.	
Anna- "why are you sad"?	
Rohan-"You know this person is writing such horrible things about me, online. He says – nobody likes me"	
Anna- " I think you should just ignore him"	Sneezy holds up the poster with " Ignore" written on it.
Sneezy- "I can't see anyone in that computer, why is Rohan upset."	Sneezy looks at the laptop and then at Rohan.
Rohan- " Now, just wait and see what I write back"	Sneezy moves from one end to the other
Anna-"Rohan, Don't do that! Haven't you heard the saying: 'Dogs bark and the caravan goes by'.	
Rohan- " Even my mother says that"!	Noise of dogs barking in the background. Everyone turns.
Sneezy- "Dirty dogs, not cool!" Achoo Achoo	Rohan holds up the poster with " Ignore" written on it.
Rohan- "I get your point Anna. This time I will ignore this comment. But what if he writes something rude again, then what will I do?"	
Anna: "Don't be friends with such people. Cut off all communication with them. If they continue to send you mean messages do not respond to them."	Sneezy holds up the placard with 'Stop' written on it
Rohan" Yes, I agree Anna. There is no point talking to a silly bully."	

Sneezy- "Bullies are sillies, Sillies are Bullies. Hey, Rohan hey Anna, that rhymes."	Anna and Rohan laugh.
Anna- "And make sure you report them to the website. Use the report button if it is available."	Sneezy holds up 'Report'.
Rohan- "But I cannot see a report button on this website".	
Anna- "Then write an email to the website."	
Rohan- "Sneezy, I am sure you don't know how to do that. Let me tell you. Every website has a Contact Us button. Click on it and write at the email id that you find mentioned there".	
Sneezy- "You know what Rohan I always report such problems to Anna".	
Rohan- (laughs) "ok".	
Anna- "Smart dog, Sneezy. Yes Rohan you must immediately talk to a trusted adult, could be your parents or your elder brother."	Anna pats Sneezy
Rohan pulls Sneezy's ears.	
Sneezy- "Stop that Rohan, Now I know what to do if someone is bullying me- Ignore, Stop and Report."	Rohan and Anna hold up placards with Ignore, Stop and Report written on them
Sneezy- "Come on, let us all go out and play in the sun. Coming with me?"	Anna and Rohan laugh and go out to play.

Activity 2. I am not a bystander!

Objective: Discussion to tell children what actions can a bystander take

Material required: Paper and pencil

Steps

1. Ask the children for any 3 reasons why they should not remain silent spectators when they notice any bullying incident, be it online or offline. Tell them that bystanders can collectively work to block a bully and weaken the bully as a bully invariably looks for support from spectators and if that is not provided to him, it is quite likely that he will backtrack a little. Tell them why it is necessary to help the victim, and remind them that by staying quiet they are harming the victim.

2. Tell children specific names of persons whom can they report to if they notice any bullying incident in school or outside school.

Conversation Starters for Parents

1. Ask a child whom would he/she report to in case of bullying? Tell the child the names of a few trusted adults, people whom you trust, so that your child knows whom to talk to in case of any trouble. Suggest a couple of options so that they know whom to approach in case you are not available.

2. Tell a child that even you have faced bullying incidents, when you were young. Tell them that you were embarrassed to talk about it to others but then you finally decided to share the incident with some trusted adults. Your grownups then gave you a solution that you could not have thought of, and how it helped you overcome the difficult situation.

Chapter 7. Privacy of Personal Information

This is a letter that we received at JaagoTeens a few months back.

Hey, my name is Alka (name changed) ..... I do not want my photo to appear in Google search results..... Please help me out......every time I type in my name, and choose Google 'image search', my photos show up. I thought deleting my Google account permanently would help, but the images did not go away. Nothing seems to work...... What can I do? please help me...Erasing these pics has become a nightmare!

Alka had uploaded some personal pictures but later wanted to delete them from the internet. The solution that we suggested to Alka can be found in this chapter.

Introduction

The problem with the internet is it doesn't let things go away. You might post something online and then delete it shortly afterwards. But you cannot be hundred percent sure that no one has seen it or copied it or shared it. This means your information might still be saved on some server in some corner of the world!

In June 2014, a very popular singer and songwriter posted a photo on Instagram of himself with his ex-girlfriend, and then "almost instantly deleted" it. Can you guess how many fans had copied and re-posted that pic?

16 million, unbelievable, but true!

Here are a few simple rules that are useful to keep in mind while one is online:

- to make proper privacy settings so that personal information is not revealed to strangers,

Privacy means to hide or conceal and not make publicly available.

- to create one's profile very carefully, without mentioning too much about family and friends, education, age, vacation plans, social plans, hobbies, interests etc. Tiny bits of information strewn all over the internet can be pieced together to get a fairly detailed idea of a person, so pay heed to the information that you are putting on the internet.

- not to put one's year of birth, only mention the date, don't worry all your birthday greetings will still get delivered to you.

- one needs to take care with pictures that one uploads, it is preferable not to upload pictures with one's house or vehicle or other belongings in the background. Revealing pictures are definitely a big no-no. The audience on the internet is unimaginably large and it is not uncommon for crooks to misuse pictures to harass or blackmail unsuspecting people.

- Do not forget to keep your online profile clean so that it does not negatively impact your future relationships, admission to good colleges and job prospects. Always remember, it is better to be safe than sorry!

- Let us take a look at why it can be risky to post personal information and what is the best way to avoid making that mistake.

Risks Associated with Posting Personal Information and Corresponding Preventive Strategies to Lower the Risk

	Personal Information	Risk	Preventive strategy
1	Real Name, School, Cellphone	Strangers could contact you because this information makes it easy to identify an individual	Put only your first name and not your full name on any online platform. Configure your privacy settings and as far as possible completely avoid uploading this information
2	Email Id	Abusive people can use it to send you spam, malware, phishing emails, links to adult sites or other unwelcome messages.	Have two email ids. One for personal use and the other while signing up for accounts that require an email confirmation
3	User Names on gaming sites, forums etc.	Avoid user names with improper words as that can invite unwanted attention.	Try and use a name that does not give out your name, age, gender, date of birth, country and does not have any indecent words in it.Don't put your full name

			as a user name, this unnecessarily discloses your identity.
4	Birthday	Young people are more likely to be harassed so it is recommended that they do not disclose their age.	Put birth date but not year of birth, this way people will still wish you on your birthday and unknown people don't get to know your age!
5	Photos and videos	1. As you grow older, the 'kiddy' photographs might be very embarrassing and there is no way you can remove them completely.	1.You could upload personal photos/videos on Google drive and then share the link with your friends. Laugh and have fun while you stay out of trouble!
		2. 'Bad' people might stalk you.	2. Do not put any semi-nude or nude pictures . Upload content that you know your family will not disapprove of.
6	Interests/hobbies/ games you play	When people talk about things that interest you, you might get so caught up in the discussion that you might forget that you don't know the person whom you are talking to.	Avoid uploading information that covers your hobbies, interests etc., it is in your best interest to share such information only with people whom you know in real life
7	Social plans/ vacation plans	There have been instances where strangers have landed up at people's birthday parties and they have had to call the police for help. People's houses have been robbed while they were away on a vacation.	Exchange such information only in private messages, calls or emails
8	Feelings/emotions /disappointments	Noticing that you are unhappy, abusers might start a conversation pretending to listen to	NEVER put your feelings online. Only share them with your friends and family members, and that too in a

		your worries very patiently. But their intent might actually be to harm you. There have been instances when such cases have ended up in sexual abuse or maybe even murders when abusers have managed to convince the victim to come and meet them in real life.	face to face conversation. Exposing a weakness in public always makes you vulnerable to exploitation so don't do this. Each of us face disappointments and there are times when we are upset, but it is critical not to share such moments with people whom we have first met online.

You're Upset, Write this on a Piece of Paper, but don't Put it Online

There is a lot of difference between writing something on a piece of paper vs posting it on the internet. You can erase the information written on a piece of paper, you might hide the piece of paper or maybe even shred it or burn it and make sure that what you wrote is gone forever.

If you are one of those who like to share all their feelings online, then you need to know that there is no guarantee that the privacy settings that work today are going to be valid at some time in future. Hence it is a good idea to avoid posting feelings and also to keep reviewing privacy settings periodically.

Photographs of Self and Family

- **Your photographs**. Remember that your cover picture and profile picture can be viewed by random people, be it Facebook, WhatsApp, or other social platforms. Avoid posting pictures that clearly identify you or your friends. Also, make sure you configure privacy settings correctly and you know what information about you is publicly visible. It is not just teenagers, often adults and senior citizens also end up posting personal information and they are not aware that it is visible publicly.

- **Photographs** *of your family*. *I have seen my own friends post pictures of their children, online. One of them had posted a picture of her small baby and she has close to 200 friends. Another friend had posted a picture of her 15-year-old daughter and she has close to 447 friends. Can my friends be sure that these pics are not being viewed by unknown people? The thought had never crossed their mind, and they immediately removed the pictures once I told them of the associated risks.*

  By making public information about our families, we might be exposing them to risk, so think twice before posting information about any family members.

What Does an ISP, Website and Browser Save Up While You Surf the Net

There is some information that you put on the net on your own but there is also some information that is constantly picked up while you browse the net. Let's see who might be saving up tiny bits of information about you.

Your ISP(Internet Service Provider) Saves

- Your IP address
- The IP address of the place that you are exchanging information with
- The time and for how long are you logged in
- Number of bytes of information that you exchange online

The Websites You Visit Save and can View

- Your IP address
- Time and duration of visit
- Text typed in
- Links clicked on

Your Web Browser Saves

- The links that you click on. If you click on 'History' in your browser you can see the websites that you have visited
- The files that you download. Clicking on 'Downloads' shows the files that you have downloaded

You could use incognito mode if you do not wish to save your browsing history (details of the sites that you visit). In incognito mode, your search history does not get saved, but this information is still available with your ISP. The website administrator also has a record of your activity on their website. It is just that your web browser does not save the history of the sites that you visit.

Answer to the Incident Related at the Beginning of the Chapter.

Hey my name is Alka(name changed)..... I want to delete my photo from Google search engine.....

Parents be cautious do not post pictures of your children, and don't put them as your profile pictures, either.

ISP is the company that provides you a connection to the internet.

Browser is the program that is used to view web pages on the internet

Please help me out......every time I search for my name, using Google 'image search', my photos show up. I thought deleting my Google account permanently will help, but the images did not go away. Nothing seems to work...... What can I do?....please help me....

Googles' support page that can be accessed at https://support.google.com/websearch/ troubleshooter/3111061?hl=en *suggests the following steps to remove content, online.*

- You can ask Google to remove your sensitive personal information, like your bank account number, or an image of your handwritten signature, or a nude or sexually explicit image or video of yours that has been shared without your consent.

- You can contact Google by filling out details at the following URL, https:// www.google.co.in/contact/

In general, if you want to remove a photo, profile link, or webpage from Google Search results, you usually need to ask the website owner (webmaster) to remove the information. Click on the image and then choose 'visit page', contact this website administrator and send them a request to remove your image.

Cookies are Okay, But You Might Want to Disable Third Party Cookies

They are small text files and not computer programs. To understand how they work let us look at an example.

Let's say you are on a shopping site and choose a couple of items and then log out. The next time when you log in, those unpurchased items show up in your shopping cart. This is possible because a cookie was sent from the shopping website to your browser when you visited it the first time. During a subsequent visit, your information is sent back to the website and your previous activity is retrieved. So the cookie brought back your earlier shopping cart.

However, third party cookies (not the website itself, but some service on it. eg. a FaceBook like button

You cannot eat internet cookies, they are files!

on some site, can send a cookie back to FaceBook) and thus can be used to offer you targeted ads. These are based on your web search and browsing pattern. You can disable these cookies from your web browser if such advertisements bother you.

Instructions would be different for each web browser. Given below are instructions on how to disable third-party cookies in Google Chrome, Internet Explorer, Safari and Firefox.

1. **Google Chrome** go to Settings/Show Advanced settings/

   At the Privacy tab click Content Settings.

   Here choose Block third-party cookies and then click Done to exit.

2. Internet Explorer

   Click on the three horizontal dots ... to get to Settings.

   Click View Advanced Settings

   Under Privacy and services search for the Cookies tab.

   Here choose 'Block only third party cookies' and exit.

3. Safari

   Choose Safari > Preferences, click Privacy, then select "Ask websites not to track me."

4. Mozilla Firefox

   Click the menu button (three horizontal bars) and choose Options.

   Next select the Privacy panel.

   Choose "Use custom settings for history" under the History tab.

   Set Accept third-party cookies to Never.

   Close the about: preferences page. Changes will be saved.

Please note that if you find that disabling third-party cookies is disrupting your normal web browsing then you might want to reverse the above changes. Experiment and see what works best for you.

Here are Some Practical Tips to Keep Your Personal Information Safe.

- **Passwords:** First and foremost, create a **strong password** and make sure you do not share it with anyone. If someone knows your password, they can access your email account/ social networking account etc, and steal your personal information. Here are a few tips on how to create strong passwords.

  Choose a meaningful phrase with 6-8 words in it, such as this, we bought our home 9 years ago

  Take the first letters and join them together. wboH9yA

Use a mix of CAPS, small letters and numbers. Add a few special characters and create a password like the one given below Wboh9yA%$

This can be your master password. For other accounts, for example for your Gmail account you might add 'GM' to the master password. This makes your password for the Gmail account, 'wboH9yA%$GM'.

Preferably write down your passwords in a notebook and keep it in a safe place. Do not save passwords on any other electronic device such as a laptop or a phone.

- **Filling out forms:** When you register for and use a site you **don't have to give them your full name**, address etc. just fill in information that you absolutely have to. Don't use your personal email id, use a general one. *Now this also means that you need to create two email ids for yourself, one for your personal use and the other for general use.*

- **Installing a new program:** At times, when you download a program and then install it you see a message cautioning you that the publisher is unknown. Make sure you still want to continue with the program because programs from unknown publishers might install malware on your system.

- **Privacy Settings:** Configure your privacy settings to prevent exposing your information on any website that asks you to create your profile. After you have made all the settings, click on 'View as Public' and make sure you are comfortable with whatever information shows up. The default privacy settings might not be good enough and your personal information might be visible publicly, so make sure you configure them according to your requirement, don't leave them at their default values.

A password provides the easiest and strongest protection for your account

- **Logging out:** Always log out of all accounts. If you use access your accounts on a smartphone, make sure you secure your phone with a password. Otherwise, if your phone is lost or stolen or someone casually picks it up, the person will have access to all of your accounts. It's unfortunate, but even known people could misuse your personal information, so make sure you secure your phone with a password.

- **Updates:** Also, make sure you have an updated antivirus program installed, the firewall is on and your operating system is updated. Regular updation is essential for protection against the latest threats.

- **Search for yourself:** Search your name on the internet and see what information shows up. If there is something you wish to remove, make sure you visit the website and delete it. If you are not able to access the information, contact the website and request them to delete this information. *"Think Before Posting any information", and keep in mind that you will not be able to delete it later on.*

- **Downloading Apps:** It is impossible to download some apps unless you provide them, virtually, full access to your phone. In such cases make sure you really need the app and if you do, then check that you are **downloading genuine apps and only download apps from reputed and trusted sources.**

It is a good idea to download apps from an official app store. Don't forget to check who is the developer of the app and also go through online reviews about the app.

Some Questions That Students Asked Us

Here are a few questions that students asked us at a JaagoTeens workshop

Q1. You say my name, address, mobile number are personal information but my father has put this information online, and it helps him in his business. Then how can it be a wrong thing to do?

Ans. It is not a wrong thing to do. Grown up people might take a decision to do so, but if you are young then it is recommended that you don't do the same. Take help from a trusted adult to help you decide what information you need to post online. Grown-ups are capable of dealing with consequences that might arise if they post personal information, but children shouldn't endanger their safety by doing the same.

Young and old people are using the same online space, but that does not mean that they can use it in the same way. Rules and limitations are not the same for children and adults.

Q2. Recently, while we were at the World Book Fair, a lady said that she received a fake email, and she thought it was from her social networking site. She clicked on the link, it took her to a look-alike page, exactly the same as her social networking site. She filled in her user name and password, but was unable to access her account. She thought there was a problem with her internet connection and logged out. A few days later, she found that she could not access her account, her password had changed, somebody had locked her out of her own account.

Ans. First and foremost, remember **not to**

- click on links sent in emails
- put too much of information on social networking sites. So, even if someone manages to gain access to your social networking account, there should not be any sensitive information that can be used to exploit you.
- The following steps can be used to delete a hacked account, an account that has been accessed by someone without your permission.

    1. Log out of all current accounts
    2. Go to this link: https://www.facebook.com/hacked
    3. Click the button "My account has been compromised"

If your Facebook account has been hacked, then delete it.

4. Search your account (type in your email address, Login name, Full Name or your specified Phone number.)

5. Enter your old password. The password that you used before your account got hacked.

6. Click the "Reset my password " button

7. If the hacker has changed your primary email address click "No longer have access to these?"

8. Now write your new email address or phone number where you want to receive the 'change password' link.

After you recover your account, you can delete the hacked account https://www.facebook.com/help/delete account

Teaching Activities

Activity 1: A Picture is Worth a Thousand Words, Really!

Objective: to explain why it is not a good idea to post pictures online, especially revealing ones, and those that depict negative behavior.

Materials required:

*   A couple of pictures that the students may have recently uploaded on the internet

*   A board and pins to pin up the pictures.

*   A paper and pen to record their responses.

Steps

1. Ask the children to walk around and see the pictures that have been pinned up on the board.

2. Next, ask them to write the information that they are able to pick out from the pictures. Teachers can drop a few hints, ask them if they can guess any of the following fields,

    -   Gender and Age

    -   Location

    -   Time of visit

    -   State of mind- happy, sad, confused

    -   Any friends or family members?

    -   What does the person do?

    -   Any hobbies/sports/interests?

    -   Does the picture depict negative behavior?

3. Keep noting down whatever they guess.

    At the end, you will find that children have been able to pick out a lot of information from a single picture. At this point, explain that a photograph reveals much more than what meets the eye!

Tell them that it is not a great idea to post pictures with negative behavior, images of a fight, or brandishing guns, or rash driving, drinking etc., because such pictures can negatively impact their job prospects, career and also their relationships in future. Such pictures leave one vulnerable to exploitation. The picture might not be shared immediately, but what if it is shared at some time in future. So, it is prudent not to share any such pictures online.

Tell them that if someone decides to upload a photo today, thinking they will delete it in future, they might be in for a rude shock when they find this impossible to do. Someone might have already copied it and shared it, so the best way to control damage is to "Think before posting anything online".

Activity 2. What is Your Personal Information?

Objective- To teach children what information constitutes their personal information.

When we talk of keeping personal information safe by configuring privacy settings, students need to know what information are we referring to.

Material required: A list of words to use in a word cloud, internet access to create a word cloud, paper for printing.

1. The following word cloud can be used as an activity. Ask children to look at the word cloud and write down on a piece of paper which item is personal.

2. Answer: Email, Photos, Address, Hobbies, Gender, Age, Sports Team, Friend's Name, Social plans, Chats, Profile, Password, School name, blog, name, mobile.

3. Discuss with children that apart from their name, address, mobile no, email id, other things such as their hobbies, interests, social plans, photographs of self, family and friends, details about friend's activities etc. should all be treated as personal information. This should not be shared freely on social platforms.

Search for personal information

4. Teachers can use any of the following websites to create a similar word cloud.

   Wordclouds.com, Wordle.net, are two popular websites used for creating free word clouds. One needs to input a list of words and then the site generates the word cloud. A Google search will lead to a number of websites that provide a platform for creation of free word clouds.

5. Children could also be given this as a home-assignment. They can draw up an exhaustive list of information that they perceive to be personal. Encourage them to take help from their parents/guardians, while creating the list. Then using one of the above-mentioned websites they can create a word cloud, save it, print it and get it to school.

Conversation Starters for Parents

1. Play our JaagoTeens Internet Safety Game- "Be a Net Smartee", and start a conversation with your child. With every roll of dice, they learn about making choices. These right or wrong choices lead to positive (ladder) or negative (snake) outcomes, simulating consequences of right or wrong online actions. Learning outcomes in this risk-free board game format makes for superior absorption of the *Fundamental Safety Rules of the Internet*. To buy the game, please visit the Amazon store and type in "Internet Safety Game JaagoTeens" and order your game right away. For bulk orders please write to us at Leena@JaagoTeens.com.

2. Urge your children and all family members to secure their accounts by configuring their privacy settings and removing personal information from it.

3. Do an activity with children, create a password with their help and check to see that it does **not** have

   - words like 'password', '1234', 'monkey', 'qwerty', 'abc123'.

   - any dictionary words

   - any personal information like your name, house no, vehicle no or your dog's name in it!

4. Assign a notebook where children write down their usernames and passwords.

Chapter 8. Online Predators

During one of our Internet Safety workshops at a school, we were addressing a crowd of students from Std 6 to Std. 9, when a young kid of class 6 asked, "Should I keep the web cam on when I am online?". A senior class student, present at the session answered his question. You can find the answer in this chapter.

Introduction

When we, at JaagoTeens, began visiting schools in 2010 and spoke to children about Interne safety, we thought it was going to be pretty easy to warn them against strangers.

However, we found that **children don't like to believe that bad people exist in the online world!**. A 13-year old student, who had more than 1000 friends on FaceBook, said almost angrily, "All strangers are not bad." We told him we agree with him. Next, we exhorted him to compare this with the real-world scenario. Are all strangers bad in the real world? He hesitatingly said, "No, they aren't". To explain our point further we asked him, "but don't your parents still caution you and say, "Don't talk to strangers on the road", "Don't take toffees from unknown people", "Don't tell a stranger where you live", etc. etc.

He seemed to now agree when we said, "we are just asking you to extrapolate the tried and tested real world advice to the online world."

Most Children have Strangers on their Friend Lists

As per a survey conducted by JaagoTeens, in some of the leading schools of Delhi, 26% students said 'Yes, they had strangers on their friend list', while, about 12 % said 'maybe', which meant that they were not hundred percent sure if they knew all the people on their 'friend list'.

Never give out details about your friend to a stranger as that can put your friend in danger.

Our survey results show that one in four children share information with unknown people when they are online. This makes it imperative for their care givers to talk to them and warn them because such interactions can entail considerable risk.

During our Workshops, We Ask Children What is the Most Common Place for them to Meet Strangers

The most common place where students of Std. 5 to 7(10-14 years) interacted with strangers was on social networking sites and online gaming sites. So, it is a good idea to talk to children who use these platforms and warn them of the risk of close interactions with people here.

How We Convinced a 13-year-old Girl that is Better to Not have Unknown People on Your 'Friend List'

A 13-year-old girl was very adamant, in spite, of having 400 friends on her friend list, that there was no risk in interacting with strangers. Nothing seemed to work, she was quite sure that there was no danger!

What we finally said seemed to make sense to her and she agreed to delete strangers from her friend list, we told her, "When you get back home today, share your friend list with your mother." She immediately retracted and said, "No". And after some time, she added, "I will remove some people from my friend list".

Mutual Friends- Is that Good Enough to be Friends with Someone?

According to a college student studying at a prominent Law college, the most commonly used criteria for adding an unknown person to one's 'friend list' is to check the number of mutual friends.

- But, it is better to avoid adding people whom you do not know yourself and whom you have not met for the first time in real life.

- Ask a couple of 'mutual friends' about the person, and only add them if you are sure

A knows B and B knows C, so A likes to think that he knows C. But, it is possible that C is just an acquaintance and not B's friend, so it is better to be friends only with people whom **you** know directly.

you are comfortable having them view your information.

Keep the Web Camera Off

A young kid of class 6 asked, "Should I keep the web camera on when I am online?".

On hearing the question, there were a lot of whispers among the senior students, and a student of Class 9 said he would answer the question.

He told his junior, "first of all, you need to know that a web cam might be remotely controlled. Someone might be able to switch your web camera on and you might not know that it is on. Secondly, don't change your clothes in front of the web cam." The young one, in a very surprised and amused tone said, 'Obviously, I won't, who does that?"

To this a few seniors in the crowd, simply whispered amongst themselves and said, "Just remember, not to do that!"

Talk to children and ask them to keep the web camera off unless they are talking to people whom they know in real life. It is safer if an adult is around while children use a web camera, even if they are talking to known individuals.

We suggest you put a piece of opaque tape over the web camera, so even if someone manages to operate it remotely they cannot infringe on your privacy.

Recognizing Signs of Perverse Behaviour

A child must talk to a trusted adult if

- the child feels weird/uncomfortable or they feel they are being followed or watched constantly by someone
- the person asks the child for a meeting
- threatens or intimidates the child in any way
- tells a child that if he/she does not give in to their demands then either they or their family will have to face some dire consequences.

Children need to be told how to recognize inappropriate behavior.

A child must certainly report to a trusted adult if he/she notices anybody indulging in any of the following:

- Makes gestures or touches themselves in a sexual manner
- Asks the victim to touch themselves in such a manner
- Sends content that is sexual in nature or sends links to pornographic sites

"I am going to meet a friend, I need to exchange a game", Parents do you know whom your child is meeting?

One needs to teach children to be mindful of whom they are meeting. Children might be so caught up in the benefit that they hoping to derive from the meeting, that they don't like to view the person, they are meeting, with suspicion. Such people could be child abusers.

At times, children might tell a grown-up very simplistically, "I am going to meet a friend, I need to exchange a game". Parents might not figure out that the child is planning to meet an 'online friend', they might assume that the child wants to meet some friend they know in real life. So, it is also important for parents to have a conversation on online safety with children and to be aware of their child's activities, both online and offline.

A parent/guardian/trusted adult must accompany a child rather than let him/her go all alone to meet an 'online' friend. The meeting should be in a public place, not a park or a shopping mall or a coffee shop or a parking lot, but in a place, that has a moving crowd of people. It might seem okay to meet in a busy market place, but make sure it is not dark and the place is not isolated or deserted and you are familiar with the place and the people in that area. Avoid locations where you need to be seated.

Do not go out to meet people whom you **first** meet online.

Don't Ignore if a Child Reports Abuse!

- It is important to never ignore any complaints that a child makes. You might not want to believe what the child is saying, but trust the child, and take swift action against the perpetrator of the offence.

- Don't forget to explain to children that **it is not their fault** if other people behave in an improper manner with them. Tell them you are glad that they have reported things to you and now they need not worry because you will handle things and make sure the harassment stops. Putting the harassment to an end is the only way to alleviate the pain of the child. This is also important for the long-term healthy development of the child.

- Parents also need to understand that as children traverses the vast expanse of the internet, they might have some awkward experiences. Assure them that if they do not hide such incidents, you would be there to help them, if required. Children need this assurance to be able to overcome any feeling of guilt that they might have. Scolding them leads to hiding of facts and that not only complicates the situation further. It is both necessary and important to support a child through such times.

A college student mentioned, that she went to meet an online friend, an unknown person, whom she was chatting with on an online dating website. She thought that she was chatting with someone her age, about 25 year-old, but this person turned out to be someone much older, close to 40. Luckily, she had gone with a group of friends and the minute she realized her mistake, she immediately left, without meeting the person.

Laws that Protect a Child

The Protection of Children from Sexual Offences Act, 2012(POCSO Act) is applicable to those below 18 years of age.

Sections 11, 13 and 15 of the Act cover Online Harassment of children and the punishment therefor.

Section 11 of POCSO Act describes what constitutes sexual harassment and the punishment for the offence.

POCSO Act protects children below 18 years of age.

Section 13 of POCSO Act gives description and punishment for use of child for pornographic purposes.

Section 15 of POCSO Act is about punishment for storage of pornographic material involving child.

Details of what each of these sections covers and the punishment therefor, can be found in Chapter 11 titled, "Laws that protect against Online Harassment".

To Lodge a Complaint with the Cyber Police

In the situation warrants police action, you may find the following information helpful:

- Ensure that offensive, criminal content has been saved up for evidence in the form of a Print screen. Click on the title bar of the window that you want to capture. Press "Alt + PrtScn". A screenshot of your currently active window will be copied to the clipboard. Paste it into your favorite image editor or document editor.

- The screen shots must have the date and time bar visible in them.

- Please note that Cyber Police will accept a complaint only when it is made in writing.

- To lodge a complaint, please visit the office of the Police in person and file your complaint.

If You are a Victim of e-mail Abuse, Vulgar e-mail etc.

Bring the following information:

- Extract the extended headers of offending e-mail find this information at:

  http://cybercellmumbai.gov.in

  html/faq/email-headers.html.

- Bring soft copy as well hard copy of offending e-mail.

- Please do not delete the offending e-mail from your e-mail box.

- Please save the copy of offending e-mail on your computer's hard drive.

Make sure you have saved up and collected all information you need to take to the cyberpolice.

If You are a Victim of Hacking

Bring the following information:

- Server Logs
- Copy of defaced web page in soft copy as well as hard copy format, if your website is defaced
- If data is compromised on your server or computer or any other network equipment, soft copy of original data and soft copy of compromised data.
- Access control mechanism details i.e.- who had what kind of the access to the compromised system
- List of suspects – if the victim is having any suspicion on anyone.
- All relevant information leading to the answers to following questions–
- what ? (what is compromised)
- who? (who might have compromised system)
- when?(when the system was compromised)
- why?(why the system might have been compromised)
- where?(where is the impact of attack-identifying the target system from the network)
- How many?(How many systems have been compromised by the attack)

  The above information is from the Mumbai Cyber Cell website. To access this information on their website, type the following URL: http://cybercellmumbai.gov.in/html/faq/information-required-for-complaint.html

- Email ids, telephone numbers and address of various cybercrime cells, of different states of India, can be found at the following website of Ministry of Electronics and Information Technology (MeitY), Govt of India: http://infosecawareness.in/cyber-crime-cell. This link can be accessed to view the information given below, it has details of the designation of the officer-in-charge, the address, telephone number and email id of the cybercrime cells of various states of India.

  1. Cyber Crime Investigation Cell

     Superintendent of Police, Cyber Crime Investigation Cell,

     Central Bureau of Investigation,

     5th Floor, Block No.3,

     Lodhi Road, New Delhi 110003

     Ph:011-24361271

     Speou9del@cbi.gov.in

  2. **Arunachal Pradesh**

Police HQ

arpolice@rediffmail.com

CID HQ

Additional DGP,CID Ulubari,

Guwahati-781007

Ph:0361-2521618

Ssp_cid@assampolice.com

3. **Andhra Pradesh**

   (i) Cyber Crime
       Police Station,
       Hyderabad City Police
       Cyber Crime Police Station,
       Web Management Team
       O/o. The Commissioner of Police,
       Hyderabad City, Basheerbagh, Hyderabad
       Ph:040-27852040,
       Cybercell_hyd@hyd.appolice.gov.in

   (ii) Cyber Crime
        Police Station,
        Cyberabad City Police
        Police Commissioner's Office
        Old Mumbai Road,Jayabheri Pine Valley,Gachibowli
        Hyderabad, Andhra Pradesh-500032
        Ph:040-27854031
        Sho_cybercrime@cyb.tspolice.gov.in

   (iii) Cyber Crime
         Police Station,CID,Hyderabad
         1/C Cyber Cell,
         3rd Floor, Crimes Investigation Department, A C,Guards, Hyderabad
         Ph:040-23307256
         cybercrimesps@cid.appolice.gov.in

   (iv) Cyber Crime Investigation Unit(CCIU)

Dy. S.P, Kotwali police station, Patna

Ph:9431818398

Cciu-bih@nic.in

4. **Gujarat**

   (i)   State CID,Crime & Rly,Gujarat State

         DIG,CID Crime,4th Floor, Police Bhavan,Sector-18, Gandhinagar

         Ph:079-23250798,079-23254931/32

         cc-cid@gujarat.gov.in

   (ii) Office of the DIG CID Crime

         Deputy Commissioner of Police, Crime

         Gaikwad Haveli,

         Jamalpur,

         Ahmedabad

         Ph:079-25330170

         Dcp-crime-ahd@gujarat.gov.in

5. **Haryana**

   Cyber Crime and Technical Investigation Cell, Gurgaon

   Old S.P.Office complex, Civil Lines, Gurgaon

   Joint Commissioner of Police

   Jtcp.ggn@hry.nic.in

   Ph:0124-2329988

   DCP Crime

   Ph:0124-2322662

   dcpcrimegrg@hry.nic.in

6. **Himachal Pradesh**

   CID Cyber Cell

   Superintendent of Police, Cyber Crime, State CID, Himachal Pradesh, Shimla-2

   Ph: 0177-2621714 Ext: 191, 0177-2627955

   cybercrcell-hp@nic.in

7. **Jammu&Kashmir**

   SSP,Crime

CPO Complex,panjtirthi,Jammu-180004

Ph:0191-2578901

Sspcrmjmu.jk@nic.in

8. **Jharkhand**

    CID,Organized Cime

    IG,CID,Rajarani Vuilding,Doranda Ranchi,834002

    Ph:0651-2491532,2444703

    agupta@jharkhandpolice.gov.in

9. **Karnataka**

    Cyber Crime Police Station,

    Additional Director General of Police (E.O.), CID, Bangalore.

    Deputy Inspector General of Police (E.O.), CID, Bangalore.

    Superintendent of Police, Cyber Crime Division, CID, Bangalore.

    Deputy Superintendent of Police (Admin), Cyber Crime Police Station, CID, Bangalore.

    C.I.D. Headquarters, Carlton House ,#1,

    Palace Road,Bangalore-560001

    Ph:+91- 080- 22094498, +91- 080- 22094564, +91- 080- 22942475, +91- 080- 22943050

    E-Mail: cybercrimeps@ksp.gov.in

10. **Madhya Pradesh**

    State Cyber Police

    IGP,Cyber Cell

    Ph:0755-2770248

    Police Radio Headquarters Campus,

    Bhadadhadaa Road, Bhopal MP

    mpcyberpolice@gmail.com

    www.mpcyberpolice.nic.in

11. **Maharashtra**

    (i) Cyber Crime

         Dy.Commissioner of Police,EOW & Cyber,

         Office of the commissioner of Police,

2, Sadhu Vawani Road Camp,
Pune-411001
Ph:020-26123346

(ii) Investigation Cell,
Pune City Police
Crimecyber.pune@nic.in

(iii) Cyber crime
Assistant Commissioner of Police,
CCPS, BKC Police Station Complex,
Mumbai   Ph:022-26504008

(iv) Investigation Cell,Pune City Police
Cybercell.mumbai@mahapolice.gov.in

(v) Cyber Crime Cell,
Thane City Police
Cybercrime Investigation Cell,
Ph:022-25429804/25424444
3rd Floor,OPP Thane Police School,
Near Kharkar Lane,
Thane(W)-400601

(vi) Cyber Crime Cell,
Nagpur City
I/C Officer – DCP
(EOW &Cyber)Ph:0712-2566766

(vii) PSI,Cyber Crime Cell,
Nagpur City,
Crime Branch,
New Administrative Building,
4th Floor, Civil Lines, Nagpur-440001

12. **Meghalaya**
SP, SCRBSP,SCRB,
Police Head Quarters,
Secretariat Hill,

Shillong-793001, Meghalaya

Meghcid2002@yahoo.com

scrb-meg@nic.in

demanjyrwa@yahoo.com

Ph:09863064997

13. **Orissa**

CID,Crime Branch

SP Crime Branch,

CID Crimes Branch Office,

Buxybazzar,Cuttack,Orissa

Pin-753001

Ph:09437450370

Sp1cidcb.orpol@nic.in

14. **Rajasthan**

Special Operations Group

Jhalana Mahal,Jagatpura Road,

Malviya Nagar,Jaipur

Ph:01412759779

splcrimejpr@gmail.com

15. **Tamil Nadu**

(i)   Cyber Crime Cell,

Commissioner Officer Campus

Egmore,Chennai– 600008

Chennai City

Ph:044-55498211

cyberac@rediffmail.com

(ii) Cyber Crime Cell,CID,Chennai

No.3, SIDCO Electronic Complex,

1 Floor, Guindy, Chennai-32

Ph:044-22502512

cbcyber@nic.in

16. **Tripura**

SP, CID SP,CID,

Arunthati nagar,

Agartala-799003

Ph:0381-2376963

Spcid-tri@nic.in

17. **Uttar Pradesh**

Cyber Complaints Redressal Cell

Agra Range 7, Kutchery Road,

Baluganj, Ph:9410837559,

Agra-232001 (UP) India

digraga@up.nic.in,

info@cybercellagra.com

18. **UttaraKhand**

Special Task force

DIG, STF,PHQ,12 Subhash road,

Dehradun, Uttrakhand 248001

Ph:9897937917

9412370272

STF OFFICE:0135-2640982

dgc-police-ua@nic.in

19. **West Bengal**

(i) CID,Cyber Crime, West Bengal

CID Cyber Crime Cell,

Bhabani Bhaban

Ph:033-24506163

occyber@cidwestbengal.gov.in

(ii) Kolkata Police Cyber Crime Police Station

ACP, Cyber Crime Police Station, Lal Bazar, Kolkata

Ph:033-22505120,033-22141420

cyberps@kolkatapolice.gov.in

(iii) North 24 Parganas Dist. Cyber Crime Cell

S.I Cyber Crime Cell,1st Floor of

Bidhannagar North Police Station,

Beside Tank No:6, Saltlake,

Kolkata-64

Ph:09836272121

20. **New Delhi**

Assistant Commissioner of Police,

Cyber Crime Economic Offences Wing,

Police Training School Complex

Malviya Nagar, New Delhi

Ph:011-26515229

acp-cybercell-dl@nic.in

21. **Chandigarh**

Cyber Crime Cell, Chandigarh

Inspector of Police, Cyber Crime Cell,

Crime Branch Office, Sector-11,

Chandigarh

Ph:0172-274280,098772281713

cybercrime-chd@nic.in

Teaching Activities

Activity 1- Puppet Show- Three Red Flags

Objective: Each of thre three red flags is a warning signal to watch out for while interacting with people online. A red flag is an indicator to a child that he/she must talk to a trusted adult.

- First Red Flag, if someone asks you to hide their conversation from grown-ups and others
- Second Red Flag, if someone sends you gifts and asks you to not let others know about the gifts
- Third Red Flag- if someone wants to interact on a web camera/asks for nude/semi-nude photographs

Children learn how to identify online abusers while they enjoy performing this skit.

Material required: The puppet show has 4 characters: Mother, Rohan (boy), Anna (girl), and Sneezy (dog). The following material will be required to make the three sock puppets that are used in this simple yet effective skit.

Material required to make the puppets

- 4 old socks

- 8 buttons for the eyes (preferably large buttons) + 1 button for Sneezy's nose
- Black wool/ yellow wool to make Mother's, Rohan's and Anna's hair.
- Felt pen or a marker pen or some black paint to draw the faces of the puppets.
- Gum to paste the buttons on the socks

Making the Puppets

Wear the sock on your hand and move your thumb so you know where the mouth of the puppet will be. Draw the mouth. Next draw the eyes and nose. Cut short strands of wool and stick to make the puppet's hair.

Puppet and dialogues	Location/Action
Mother Girl- Anna Sneezy	At Anna's house.
Anna- Mumma, you know what Pratira has been talking to an online friend for a long time.	
Mother- Who, Pratira, that shy girl in your class, she is so quiet…	
Anna- Yes, yes that Pratira.	
Mother- Do her parents know about this?	
Anna- No. Her online friend, Andy has told her not to tell anybody.	
Mother- And what if she tells somebody?	
Anna- No she can't, you won't understand. It's a pinky promise!	
Mother- Sneezy, go and get a red flag. Anyone asks you to keep things secret ,then you need to be alert.	
Sneezy- me, achooachoo. But, I always tell Anna everything!	
Anna- I know that Sneezy, but probably you should stop telling me how many times you sneeze in a day.	
Anna- but Mumma, Andy has given her so many nice gifts. He is very kind to her and listens to her problems. Pratira likes to talk to him.	
Mother- Anna, another red flag for accepting gifts from people. Sneezy, go and get a red flag.	

Sneezy- Achoo. So, this means no bones from strangers?	Sneezy throws away a gift- wrapped bone.
Anna- Andy is not a stranger!	
Mother- Even if you have known someone for a long time, you still cannot accept gifts from online friends.	
Anna- Andy's nice but there is something I don't like about him.	
Sneezy- he's asked Pratira for gifts?	
Anna- No Sneezy. Mumma he just asked Pratira to send a photograph of hers. That's all! But she was very upset the whole day.	
Mother- did you see the photograph?	
Anna- No, she did not show it to me, though Pratira shares all her secrets with me.	
Mother- Another red flag Sneezy. Never send a photograph of yours. I have read in the newspapers that at times people might pressurize children to send a nude photograph of themselves.	
Sneezy- Anna let us go to Pratira's house. I think she needs our help.	
Mother- Smart dog, Sneezy. Let's go! We need to immediately inform her parents.	
Anna- do you think we should tell the police also?	
Mother- Her parents will do that.	
Anna- If you think a friend of yours needs help then don't wait, reach out to them!	

Conversation Starters for Parents

Children might not always respond, so don't try to prod them too hard. Simply listen to whatever they might say.

1. You could ask children, "Do you know that online predators exist on the internet?" Explain who a predator is and content from the above chapter can be used for this purpose.

2. Ask children, "Do you think children, younger than you, need to be told to avoid having conversations with strangers?". Then continue the conversation once they respond.

3. Tell children that at times people might try to have a conversation that is sexual in nature. Tell them not to continue with the conversation and to leave the website immediately.

4. Discuss with your child that anything inappropriate or unnerving, on the internet, must be reported to you.

5. Tell a child about online grooming, wherein an online predator(pedophile) might interact with a youngster for a fairly long period of time. They might work to make the victim feel confident and comfortable with them, showing a lot of concern for what they think, how they feel, what they want etc. Tell children to be always wary of such people and stop all conversation or interactions with such people.

"Oh, simply ban children from using the internet", is an oft-heard statement from parents, teachers, educators. But, why we at JaagoTeens feel that blocking/banning a child's online activities might not be the best way to keep a child safe

-   Did you stop crossing the road or driving a car due to the rise in the number of road accidents in recent years? You didn't, because you couldn't have. Similarly, one cannot stop using the internet because soon it will be very closely intertwined with people's lives and their day to day activities. The solution will lie in using the internet sensibly rather than not using it at all.

-   The internet can be accessed through many different devices, a computer, a mobile phone, a tablet, a TV, a game console etc. If you ban a child from using the internet on one device, they might end up using it on some other device, and that too without your knowledge, so it is better that you monitor and not ban their online activities.

-   Children love to be a part of their peer group, and to talk about current things, taking away the internet from them might make them feel frustrated and discouraged.

-   Makes it more difficult for them to share bad experiences. Talking to children about the internet is a great way in which parents can be a part of their online lives, and that too without being too intrusive. This encourages them to share their experiences, both good and bad, with a parent/trusted adult.

-   The online world also helps children develop a lot of real-world life skills, for instance, building trustworthy friendships, practicing advocacy and empathy, not getting swayed by false propaganda/trash/rumours/lies etc., skills that come in handy in the real world and help them cope better in the real world.

-   Children, at a young age, are not able to perceive or sense danger while indulging in various risky activities. They might not be able to fully understand why their parent is blocking their internet activity. It might be more effective if a parent/ trusted adult has a conversation with them where he/she explains the risks, what the parents fear, and why a child should tell them about anything they find disturbing, in this way, both, parent and child can enjoy surfing the net together.

- Today children need access to be internet to complete their school projects. If they find that access is being blocked, they might lie about the reason for being online, which can make things difficult both for a parent and a child. Building an atmosphere of healthy and open conversation is the best way to ensure a child's safety and well-being.

Chapter 9. Smartphone Safety, Your Phone Isn't Smart, But You Are!

I gave my phone to a local repair shop. The repair man asked me to come and collect it in an hour's time. I didn't have much to do and was back at the shop in about 20 minutes. I was shocked to find him happily scrolling through all the pictures on my phone. What should I have done before I gave the phone at the repair shop?

Find the answer to this question in this chapter.

Introduction

Your smartphone is like a mini-computer, it lets you surf the internet, call and message your near and dear ones, and run dozens of apps as you effortlessly glide and tap your fingers over the touch screen.

These technological advancements make things so much more convenient and life so much simpler that we don't like to think of any risks associated with them.

Here's a list of 12 simple tricks that will shield you and keep you out of harm's way, while you keep discovering new fun things to do with your smartphone!

Use a Password or Pin on Your Phone

1. Keep a strong password, and not something as simple as "1234", don't use something that can be guessed very easily.

2. To set up a password take these steps:

    (a) For an iPhone

    Go to Settings > Touch ID & Passcode. On devices without Touch ID, go to Settings > Passcode:

    Tap Turn Passcode On.

    Enter a six-digit passcode. ...

    Enter your passcode again to confirm it and activate it.

    (b) For an Android phone

    To get to the security options, tap the menu button from the home screen, then choose Settings>Security>Screen lock. (The exact words may vary slightly from phone to phone.)

    (c) For a Windows Phone 8

    From the home screen, tap Settings, and then select lock

screen.Scroll down to "Password". To set a password for the first time, slide the "Password" bar to On.

Enter your new password in the "New password" field, and then re-enter it in the "Confirm password" field. Tap done.

The instructions vary from one phone model to another, so do not hesitate to take help from a smart youngster if you are finding it difficult to set a password on your phone. Or simply type "how to set password + make and model of your phone" into a search engine. Then follow the set of instructions that show up.

If you are wondering why do I need a password on my phone, here's why.

If your phone is lost/stolen or a person casually picks up your phone, the trespasser might gain access to your messages, pictures, videos and any apps that you might not have signed out of. Your e-mail, LinkedIn, Whatsapp account, various social networking accounts, e-wallets, banking or shopping sites might all be accessible to an intruder. Thus, to keep both, your personal information and financial information safe, the simplest line of defense is to use a password on your phone.

A JaagoTeens Survey of 100 college students, of Delhi, in the 19-21 years' age group revealed that about 76% female students and 73.3 % male students used password protection on their phones. The combined average, which means irrespective of gender, of those using a password was 75%.

Next, we asked the same group of college students if their parents used passwords, on their phones. According to the results of the survey, we found that only 40% of their parents used passwords, with 35% of mothers and about 43% of fathers securing their phones with passwords.

The response was not completely unexpected. The current generation of college students have been using smartphones since they were young kids, and are aware that someone might misuse their smartphone. The older, landline generation, treats a smartphone as a device to make calls from, and find setting passwords a cumbersome process. But, it is advisable to set passwords on smartphones as there might be a lot of personal information on your phone.

Do you have this information saved with you, you need it if you want your stolen/lost phone?

You need to know the

- manufacturer
- model number,
- and unique device identification number (either the IMEI), also known as the Mobile Equipment Identifier (MEID) number.

Make sure you find out all of the above information, write it down, and keep it in a safe place. If you can give the IMEI number to your service provider they can block the handset, which means it cannot be used even with another sim.

*To find your **IMEI no key in** *#06#. Your IMEI number will be displayed. Write it down in a file. Don't store it on your computer, laptop and certainly not on your phone. If your phone is lost the IMEI number will also be gone.*

Sending your phone to the repair shop or if you are planning to give away your old phone

Here is the answer to the question that we asked at the beginning of the chapter:

I gave my phone to a local repair shop. The repair man asked me to come and collect it in an hour's time. I didn't have much to do and was back at the shop in about 20 minutes. I was shocked to find him happily scrolling through all the pictures on my phone. What should I have done before I gave the phone at the repair shop?

Before you give your phone for repair/service

(a) Make sure you log out of all apps. Back up all messages including your Whatsapp messages, personal photos, videos, on to your computer/laptop and remove them from the phone, delete anything that you don't want unknown people to view. There have been instances when a phone was given for repair, and the people there accessed and misused photographs/videos/messages etc. The onus lies with the owner of the phone to remove sensitive information from it.

(b) Also, clear the browsing history. You need to clear cache so that any account information does not remain saved in it. Instructions will be different for an Android, Windows or an iPhone so check online for step by step instructions on how to remove this. Type "Clear Cache "+ "the make of your phone" into a search engine. Then follow the instructions given on the screen.

(c) Banking websites, like ICICI Bank, suggest that before you hand-over your phone for repair, contact your bank and request them to block your mobile banking applications. When you get your mobile back, request the bank to unblock it.

(d) Don't rush to give your phone, think through all the different things that you might need to remove, do that patiently, and only then hand over your phone to the repair shop.

If you are planning to give away your phone to someone, or donate it, or exchange it

(a) Back up the data on your phone. Instructions for Android, Apple and Windows phone are different. Type 'how to take a backup my _____ (manufacturer and make) phone' into a search engine. Follow the instructions that are displayed by the search engine.

(b) Remove and keep your SIM card with you, don't give it away.

(c) Erase all data on your SD card.

(d) Remove and keep your micro SD card, don't give it away.

(e) Most importantly, do a factory reset.

(f) In case you are planning to get a new mobile number, then do not forget to let your bank know that your mobile number has changed.

(g) If you are planning to give away or sell your iPhone, iPad or iPod touch there could be the following possibilities. You still have your device or you don't have the device because you have given it away.

- If you have your device, you should remove all your personal information from it. But don't erase your contacts, photos, documents etc. while you are signed into iCloud with your Apple Id. That will remove all such information from the server and from all other devices that might be signed into iCloud.

- If you have given away the device, you could either ask the new owner to erase the data or change your Apple Id. For detailed instructions, you need to visit Apple's support page and follow the instructions given there.

Just a tiny profile pic, stop and think, the information it gives away can be Brobdingnagian

Avoid using profile pictures that identify you clearly. Using a name and picture, more information can be gathered online, hence it is preferable to use a generic image or to use a picture that does not show your face very distinctly.

Good and Bad of Location Services

If you wish to share your location, you need to turn on Location Services on your smartphone. Be sure you know which apps are using your location and if you are okay with it.

- In case your phone geotags your photos, and you don't want that to happen, then make sure you turn this feature off. The geotag provides the date, time and place where the picture was clicked.

- Use caution while 'checking in' on FaceBook. It might be fun to make your friends jealous that you are enjoying a movie but, thieves might get to know that you are not at home, and can rob your house.

- Location information can be added to tweets sent from Twitter, if you want others to know where are you tweeting from. However, be very careful, and mention your location only if it is an essential requirement of the tweet.

- Be cautious while using services like Foursquare that use your location. It is dangerous to let the whole world know your exact location. You might think that you have shared your location with just your friends, but if your FaceBook and Twitter account are also linked with your Fousquare account, you might end up broadcasting your location to people who could stalk you and cause you harm.

- There are some applications for which you need to have the Location on. If you are using Google Maps, to reach a new address, then you need to keep the location services on.

- Location services can be useful to track loved ones.

- The settings vary from one model to another, so if you face any difficulty in configuring the above features, type the feature followed by the make and model of your phone. Then follow the instructions that show up in the search engine.

Either Accept Full List of Permissions or Quit

Many a times, you might have wondered if you should accept all the permissions the app is asking for, or should simply quit. Don't be impatient, don't download an app unless you go through the information given on the screen.

- Read the description and the content rating.

- Read reviews by other users.

- Look for more information on the app developer.

- If people have said it is malware infested, then do not download it.

- Always download apps from trusted sources. Don't randomly click download links. Be careful of attachments received in emails, do not click on them.

- Make sure you have an updated operating system.

- Watch out for what information an app might be collecting and with whom they could be sharing this information. If you are not too sure what do some permissions mean, do an online search and see if you are comfortable sharing that information.

Bluetooth- When Not in Use, Disable It

- Blue tooth uses wireless technology that allows transfer of data between devices, this does not require actual connection with a USB cable,

- One needs to turn off blue tooth when not in use, else it can be used by criminals to access data on your phone or to guess your location.

- Keeping blue tooth off also protects you against incoming malicious codes, if your Bluetooth is on malware can get installed on your phone.

Never accept a phone, as a gift, from a person you have first met online

- If the gift is to be kept a secret, or

- if the person gifting the phone asks you to keep all conversations private, or
- if the person threatens you with dire consequences if you let others know about the phone, the intentions of the person are suspect and do not trust such a person.

The person might indulge in conversations that are indecent, and then might try and insist on a real-life meeting with the intention to sexually abuse the receiver of the gift. So, ask children to be careful and to never accept a phone as a gift, however tempting the offer might sound. Reiterate to them that things that are too good to be true are the ones that one needs to view with suspicion and to always tell you if they come across something that they are unsure of.

Your phone is lost/stolen, how to disable access to your email and other social networking accounts, on that phone?

Log in with your laptop or some other device. Change passwords for all your accounts. This will prevent the thief from signing into your accounts through your phone. But you need to act very fast!

Be careful, particularly, when you are going to a crowded market or to a place where you have heard that mobile theft is pretty common. Try and secure your phone with a cord/string rather than simply place it in your pocket, jacket or backpack.

Lodge an FIR. Don't ignore this step, as the onus to report loss lies with the owner of the phone.

Is your password, account details or ATM pin stored on your smartphone?

Do not store any of the above information on your phone, make sure you delete it from your phone, in case you already have it stored. In case your phone is lost or stolen, then this information can easily be misused. Don't keep it in messages/mails either. Preferably, write your passwords and other banking information in a notebook and put this away in a safe place at home. This old way of storing personal information is a tried and tested way and can still be used to keep your information safe!

Remember **not to** store passwords or other financial information on any other electronic devices, either.

WEP vs. WPA and free WiFi networks

Check what encryption does the WiFi network for your home connection use. Click on the WiFi tab on your smartphone and check what security does it use. The steps to do this will vary with the make and model of your phone so search online for "how to find my wifi security encryption, followed by the make and model of your phone".

WEP encryption is not very strong, it can be easily cracked so it might not be a good choice. In terms of providing a more trustworthy connection, WPA is better and WPA2, is the best. Being less secure means that someone can intercept the information that you send and receive over the internet; intruders might be able to read your passwords, credit card information, messages etc.

JaagoTeens Survey

We asked 50 college students if they accessed personal accounts, like email or social networking sites, on public WiFi.

Their responses revealed that about 43 % students accessed personal accounts on public Wifi. They used the free wifi services at locations such as those available at coffee shops, universities, airports, etc.

- 43% said "Yes, they do access personal accounts on public WiFi"
- 40 % said, "No, they don't access personal accounts on public WiFi"
- 17 % said, "They might occasionally access personal accounts on public WiFi".

Now why do we consider this risky?

Very often, such networks might not be secure, they might have been hacked and a user's information might be intercepted by cyber criminals. It is best to avoid accessing personal accounts, like an email account or a social networking accounts and to avoid sending financial information over such public wifi networks. Such networks can be used to surf the net or to search for general information.

Hackers sometimes create wifi networks that have names that sound similar to popular networks. People might not notice the small difference in the name. If they connect to such networks their data can be stolen so it is better to avoid public wifi especially for financial transactions.

If one must access one's personal accounts one has to either wait till one can use a private wifi connection or else use a 2G/ 3G network on one's phone. These networks are secure as they use data encryption so even if the data is intercepted it cannot be deciphered.

My friend could not get her late mother's pictures back!

While we were writing this chapter, one of our friends lost her phone. What hurt her the most was she had pictures of her late mother on the phone, and now she knew she would never get them back.

She was worried about a couple of other pictures on her phone, particularly that of her daughter and niece, she just hoped that no one would misuse them.

It is a good idea to back up your contacts and pictures, videos etc. on to some other device like a laptop, computer, tablet or maybe even an old phone. In this digital age, when we no longer maintain hand written telephone diaries, the moment your phone is lost, your entire list of contacts is gone. You might not be able to recall the numbers of your near and dear ones because people are no longer in the habit of memorizing phone numbers.

Keep removing personal pictures/messages/videos, regularly, from your phone, you could store them on a back-up device if you need to keep them, else you can delete them. This gives you space on your phone and in case your phone is lost/stolen you will not be upset about your lost contact details, photos, videos and messages.

Can your antivirus be your policeman?

In case the phone is lost/stolen, an antivirus can help locate the phone. It can also be used to remotely lock the device and erase data on the phone. Now this can be a lot of relief for the user.

Antivirus also protects you against harmful viruses, malware, spyware and text messages and keeps your personal data safe.

Keeping the operating system (eg. Android, iOS, Windows), applications and browsers (eg. Chrome, Opera etc.), updated because security patches protect you against the latest threats.

The following url provides a complete list of precautionary steps that the police ask you to take to protect yourself against mobile theft. http://zipnet.in/ safety tips for mobile phone use.htm

Chapter 10. Modes of Digital Payments and Safe Online Payments

This incident was narrated to us by a 20-year-old college student.

Her friend was fascinated by some online shopping site called 'Zoomik'. She was thrilled to find them offering a free hair straightener worth Rs. 1000/- with the portable charger worth Rs.2000/-, that she was purchasing. While placing the order, she filled in all details, including her name, address etc. and then paid online to complete the transaction. She kept waiting but did not receive her order and Rs.2000/- was debited from her bank account.

What were the warning signals that she skipped noticing? Read on and find the answer in this chapter.

Online banking is a very convenient feature to use, you can do your banking and other financial transactions, without having to step out of your house. But, if you feel anxious, and are always wondering if you have done things correctly, you are not alone. Go through the tips given here, see if they help you understand how to avoid trouble while making online financial transactions.

In each of the points discussed below, a particular aspect of online safety has been taken up. We have also discussed various modes of digital payment, knowledge of these modes enables one to be a part of a cashless society, something that the Government of India is working towards post demonetization.

Keep a Strong Password

Keep a **strong password,** use at least 8 characters and make it a mix of small letters, cap, numbers and special characters. Think of a phrase and use the first letters to build your password. This will also help you remember it. For example - "I **w**alk 5 km every day" and your password could be iW5kmeday@@. If you are wondering how to memorize the special characters you can think of @, @ as your shoes!

- Write your passwords in a notebook and keep it in a safe place.
- Don't store passwords on any device.
- Don't keep dictionary words as passwords as they can be cracked quite easily, even if the word has a very difficult spelling.
- Passwords, like '1234' or a blank or 'password' or your name, dob, your dog's name etc., are not difficult to guess.

Make sure you do not share your password with anyone at all. Don't have the same password for all your accounts, otherwise, if one password gets leaked all your accounts can be hacked into.

Do Not Click on Links Received in Emails/messages

Always access your banking site by typing in the URL, and not by clicking on any links sent to you in mails/messages/chats. These links can lead you to spoof sites or phishing sites. Spoof sites are fraudulent websites that can download malware on to your system, if you happen to click on them. Phishing websites trick you into providing your financial information and cyber criminals can use this information to steal your money.

A lady once told us that she received a link in her mailbox, it appeared to be from her bank. The instructions given in the mail, asked her to click on the link present in the mail. She clicked on the link and a page that looked exactly like her bank's page opened. It had the same color combination, logos etc, and she did not suspect that she was on a fake website. She entered her user name and password to access her account but found that her account did not open.

After a few days, she discovered that she had been locked out of her bank account. The thieves had accessed her account and then changed the password. But luckily, it was a dormant account with very little money in it. She feared that the same thing could have happened with her active account.

So, the moral of the story is to be careful and aware that a link received in an email could lead you to a fraudulent website or it could download malware on to your system.

If your email service provider, eg. Yahoo, Gmail etc, have marked an email as spam, then be extra cautious if you decide to still follow a link received in the mail.

I Got Fooled by this Spam Link, Learn to Recognize Obvious Signs!

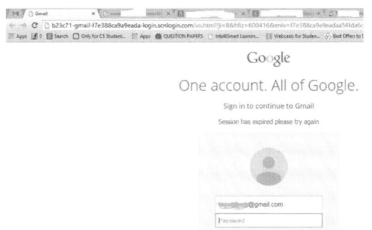

I got fooled and thought that this link, in my mail box, was from my Gmail account, so I clicked on a 'bad' link and you can see that it has asked me to sign into my Gmail account with my username and password. The moment I would have done that, my password would have been saved by this fake website and those 'thugs' would have gained access to my email account.

Now why did I guess that this website could be a 'cloned' one. Look at the url.

Compare it with the usual Google sign- up url that looks like this:

> 🔒 https://accounts.google.com/Login?hl=en

- The real website, has a green padlock,
- the url starts with https, implying it is a secure connection, and not simply http and
- the link says 'accounts.google.com'.

Take a look at the spam link above, all of the above are absent, so one can guess that it must be a spam link.

Mouse over on a Link

Another safety instruction to follow is to make sure one knows where a link will take one to. Do a 'mouse over' the link, do not click on it. See what does it reveal as the target in the status bar at the bottom of the window. If it is simply a combination of a large number of characters, and you don't seem to recognize it, avoid clicking on the link

Do not save any financial information on your computer/ phone.

Do not save any financial information, like your credit card number, CVV number, ATM pin, username and passwords, or other account information, anywhere on your computer or your mobile phone.

The good old way of writing these down in a notebook and putting the notebook away in a safe place, is still the safest way to store such information.

Someone known to you might see the information on your computer/phone and might be tempted to misuse it, so avoid storing any sensitive financial information on these devices.

If you need to give your laptop/phone etc. for service or for repair all of your data, including your banking information, can be misused at the shop. If your laptop has crashed, it is quite likely that you cannot access any information on it and it is not possible for you to delete sensitive information from it. Hence, as a habit, it is better not to store financial information, or passwords for banking sites, on any of your electronic devices.

Do not save banking passwords in your browser

Do not save passwords for banking, email, or social networking sites in your browser. If you are on a public computer, be very sure that you do not choose the remember/save passwords option. In case you feel that you have mistakenly saved the password, make sure you go back and delete it.

The steps to delete the saved password will depend on the browser that you are using, and instructions will be different for each browser.

To find the instructions on how to remove saved passwords follow these steps:

Type "removing saved passwords in (write the name of the browser that you are using, is it Internet Explorer or Chrome or Safari etc,)" into the search box. Then follow the instructions that show up on the screen to remove the saved password.

Saving passwords is a convenient option to use, but it also has an associated risk. As a standard practice never allow the browser to save your passwords for sensitive accounts eg.a banking website, social networking website or any other place where you have personal information stored. Let's say someone uses the browser after you, and you were signed into your banking account, they can straight away go into your banking account, and might steal your money.

If you happen to be away for a short while, and your system in on, then anyone using your system, can gain unauthorized access to your account.

If your laptop or phone is lost or given for repair, and you have saved your passwords in the browser, a third person can gain access to your personal accounts.

Install an Antivirus on Your System

If you noticed some or all of these things happening to your system, you need to sit up and take notice because your system might be infested with malware.

- Your browser changes to something different, and you are very sure you did not make that change
- You see new tool bars, but did not add them
- Windows stops working properly and doesn't seem to respond.
- Your computer is running much slower than normal, and your usual programs take much longer to load
- Your hard disk light seems to be on a lot more than it normally is, with the hard disk making a continuous noise.

First and foremost, without any further delay, install an antivirus on your system.

Download a free antivirus program from the internet or buy a paid version and run the program to scan your system.

The antivirus program will remove the malware that might be present on your system.

You need protection against future attacks. This can be achieved by having an updated antivirus program. It is better to have the 'automatic update' option selected, so that the program gets updated when you are connected to the internet. This will protect your system against future threats.

Keep Your Operating System Updated

Keep your operating system updated, when you go online, allow the system updates to happen. *Do not disable updates*.

An update might be available in case the developers

- have detected some inadequacy in the software, probably a loophole, that might be allowing malware to enter the system, or
- there are some errors in the operating system, or
- there are some new features that the creators wish to add,

Allowing the system to update takes care of all of the above. An operating system is, after all, a piece of software, so it needs updating to provide full functionality in a continuously changing online environment.

Keep Bluetooth off when not in use

Learn to recognize how to turn Bluetooth on and off on any device that you use.

And why is this important to know?

If your Bluetooth is on, you might receive unsolicited messages or a cybercriminal might be able to see sensitive information on your Bluetooth enabled device.

So, after you have used the Bluetooth feature, make sure you turn it off.

Do not use a rooted device for Online Banking

Do not jailbreak (iPhone) or root (Android device) your mobile phone, if you plan to use it for online banking. If you've already rooted your phone, probably to install some games or apps, then you need to know that such a device is more vulnerable to malware attacks than an unrooted device. Your safety might be compromised, so do not make online financial transactions with this device.

Recognising Phishing Emails

Phishing emails might be detected by

- by their sense of urgency, asking you to send some information immediately, along with a threat that if you do not update your information then, you will stand to lose money or something will go wrong etc. The thieves know that if you stop and think, you will not fall into their trap so they want you to act fast, without thinking.
- They promise to deliver very large sums of money. Remember the age-

old rule, 'no one will ever give you something, for nothing'. So never-ever believe such mails.

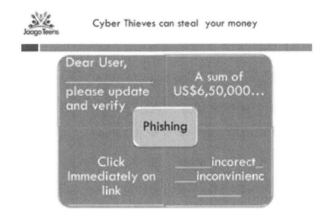

- Links received in emails, never click on these links, they will ask you to enter your user name and password and once you have done that they will save your information and then use it to steal your money.

Mails that have spelling mistakes/poor grammar are a big give-away. It is quite likely that the mail is from a phishing website.

If you are not sure that the mail you have received is genuine or spam, copy some portion of the email into the search box of your search engine and hit the search button. If the mail is a scam, it is quite likely that it has been reported by people. If you find that it has been reported by others, simply delete the mail, count yourself as lucky that you did not choose to answer the mail and just ignore all such mails, in future.

Log Out of Your Banking Account

After you have completed an online financial transaction, make sure you log out. Do not simply close the browser, log out, and then close the browser.

Never save banking passwords on your computer, and never on a mobile phone.

If someone else uses the computer or phone, after you, they might get full access to your bank account. Also, when a phone is lost or stolen remember to inform your bank so that you can be alerted if any unauthorized transactions are made from your account.

Caution While Entering Your ATM Pin

If you are typing in confidential information in a public place be careful about people who might be prying around. Make sure you cover up the keypad while punching in your pin number.

Another fraud involves installing ATM skimming devices which are often very difficult to detect, the thieves fix a card reader on the genuine card slot. This then skims card details from the magnetic strip on the back of a card. It also has a false keypad or pinhole camera to record digits that the user is typing in. Make sure you activate the SMS feature for your account so that you know immediately if anyone happens to make unauthorized transactions with your ATM card.

In case you have not already activated the SMS feature, visit your bank and ask them how you to activate the 'SMS alerts' feature. There is generally a nominal fee for this feature but it is useful as it alerts you against any withdrawals made from your account.

The procedure is a little different for each bank, but activating this feature, can save you from a lot of heart-ache.

Share Any Bad Online Experience with Others

Share any incident of scamming with friends, family as well as other online communities. Awareness is the key to fight cybercriminals.

The moment you share an experience, there is someone who would invariably have something similar to share and will tell you, "Listen, even I got a mail like that and this is what I did ….".

This helps protect more and more people against fraud and cheating, so go ahead and share any bad online experiences with others.

Safe Shopping Tips

1. Do not buy from unknown retailers, even if the offer looks very good and tempting.

2. Search for customer reviews, read what have people said about this product and a couple of more products on the same website. Search for some reviews about the website, so that you know the reviews are genuine.

3. When you swipe your credit card, the purchase is added to your

outstanding balance and you have to clear it by the end of the month. In case of a debit card, the money is immediately earmarked in your account, and is not available to you the moment you make a payment. For making online payments, it is better to use a credit card rather than a debit card because they have better fraud protection.

4. It is better to use a home wi-fi connection or if you are outside, preferably use a 2G/3G internet connection, and not a free wi-fi hotspot, especially, when you are making a payment.

Answer to Shopping Scam Mentioned at the Beginning of the Chapter

This incident was narrated to us by a 20-year-old college student.

Her friend was fascinated by some online shopping site called 'Zoomik'. She ordered a portable charger for Rs.2000/- with which they promised a free hair straightener, worth 1000/-. While placing the order she filled in all details, including her name, address etc. and then paid online to complete the order.

She kept waiting but did not receive her order. Rs.2000/- were deducted from her account, against the transaction.

Warning signals:

- She had not heard of the shopping site, but she did not try to verify the credibility of the website by searching about it, online or checking with some friends or family members.

- The offer was too good to be true. With a charger, worth 2000/-, she was getting a hair straightener, worth 1000/- free!

- Then she filled in her financial information on a fake website, without knowing if the online shopping site was genuine.

- She should have immediately informed her bank about the fake transaction and got her card blocked to prevent any further transactions.

- She did not tell her parents that she had made a wrong payment and lost some money!

Job, Internship and Scholarship Scams and a Preventive Strategy for all Such Situations

Case I is about a fake internship offer to a college student.

Case 2 is about a fraudulent home-based data entry job offer made to a house wife.

Case 3 is a false job offer to a job-seeker.

Case 4 is about a fake scholarship offer.

Case 1. Fake internship offer: A student applied for an online internship, she got selected and was appointed to work as an HR intern. Her work was to conduct telephonic interviews and to later report to the company with tables, graphs, and detailed analysis of the responses that she had gathered. She worked for about 25 days. All of a sudden, the company stopped replying to her emails and phone calls. And, of course, she did she get any certificate of internship from the company.

Case 2. **Data entry job offer**: A young housewife wrote to us saying that she saw an advertisement of Sigma Info Tech about a home- based data entry job that asked her to initially pay a security deposit of Rs.3000/-. She wrote to us saying, "I really need this job. I don't know whether it is fake or real so will you please tell me how can I check?"

Case 3. **Job offer at a reputed company:** The following was reported by a young person, who was super-excited, when he got his first job offer: "I received a call from recruixxx2naukri.com on 18/03/2015 saying I was eligible for a job offer in a reputed Motor company. They had seen my profile and shortlisted me for an HR interview. When I received the call, there was a lot of noise in the background, and I thought the call was being made from a call center."

He wrote, "They asked me to pay Rs.2246/- as registration fee. I searched for them on Google to check if the website existed and found that the email id was genuine. Registration fee seemed reasonable, so I paid it."

"At the next level, they asked me, on 19/03/2015, to pay three installments of Rs. 7,864/-, Rs.10,111/-, and Rs.14,605/-. They said this was a security deposit and it would be returned by cheque, after the HR interview, in case I failed the interview. If I was selected, then this amount will be refunded after I complete one month at the job."

"Unfortunately, I paid these amounts. Now they have stopped responding to all telephone calls and emails."

Case 4. Scholarship offer: In a case of phishing, an email invitation was received by a student asking her to register on a portal to collect her scholarship. The girl immediately registered for the written test. She was asked to make an online payment as the registration fee for the test. She followed all the steps and made an online payment. Later on, she found out that the website was fake and was meant for phishing and the same modus operandi had been used to dupe a lot more students.

Preventive Strategy

In all of the above situations or in similar situations, we suggest the following checks could have been used. Fraudsters are always thinking of new ways to dupe people so the key is to stay alert and to share such incidents with other people.

- First and foremost, if any website asks you to pay money the likelihood of its being fraudulent is extremely high. So, one needs to tread with caution and not keep things secret, talk about the offer to friends, family members and start searching online if such offers have been made to others and if they are genuine. Check the reputation both, of the recruiting company and the company that has made the job offer. Often, the name of the recruiting website is very close to a well-known website, and there are high chances that it is a scam website

- There are a number of websites where you can check whether a particular website is a scam website. One such website is scamadviser.com. Do a search online for "check if website is scam" and then input the name of the website to check how trustworthy does it appear to be.

- You will see from the above examples that generally one is targeted with offers based on what one is most likely to fall for. They also indicate that fraudsters generally study the behavior and requirement of their target audience.

- Call up the recruiting company directly, and ask if they are hiring through any such recruitment agency. Verify from the company if the recruiting website is genuine and ask if they have been authorized to collect money from candidates who will be appearing for the job interview.

- Most reputed companies generally do not ask for any security deposit before an interview so do not delay making this call.

- If you feel that you have made a payment to a fraudulent website, immediately lodge a complaint with the cyber police of your area. Give all details to them. *Even if the amount lost is small, make sure you lodge a complaint.*

- To avoid such situations, ensure that you do not leave too much information about yourself on social networking sites etc. Be careful while posting information on social networking sites, make sure your privacy settings have been configured with care, and you do not have unknown people on your friend list. You can see that students received mails with offers for internships, scholarships. An older age group received emails for jobs etc so the tricksters had some idea of the profile of those whom they had targeted.

- Most importantly, talk to a trusted friend/adult and do not panic but take appropriate action.

Digital Payments

Introduction

Digital payment is a mode of payment that does not involve hard cash, it uses an electronic means to fulfil the transaction. According to NPCI, (National Payments Corporation of India) currently about 92% of payments, in India, are made with cash and only about 8% are through electronic means. But, with the current thrust on cashless payments, this proportion is set to change. To be able to adopt a cashless mode of payment, a large proportion of people will have to learn these new modes of payment.

Here we have discussed some payment methods.

First and foremost,

What you need to do:

1. Open a Bank Account.
2. Link your mobile number with your bank account.

   Linking your mobile number with your account will allow you to use *99# services. This linking can be done either by visiting your bank, or through your bank's ATM or through internet banking.
3. Link Aadhar number with your bank account.

Aadhar is the unique identification number issued by the Unique Identification Authority of India (UIDAI). Linking of Adhaar number can be done either by visiting your bank, or through your bank's ATM or through internet banking. It allows you to use AEPS (Aadhar Enabled Payment System).

Different Modes of Digital Payment:

1. Banking cards

Banking cards are primarily of three types ,pre-paid cards, debit cards and credit cards.

Pre-paid cards are similar to prepaid mobile phone cards. All you have to do is buy a card, load it with the desired amount and the card is ready to be used. You do not require to be an account holder of the bank that issues this card.

(sidebar) Digital payment involves making a cashless transaction

(sidebar) For opening a bank account one needs to provide proof of identity and address

Debit and Credit cards are issued by the bank to its account holders. To be able to transact with them one requires a Bank Account, the debit card/credit card and a PIN issued by the bank. Activation of the PIN can be a little different for each bank so check with your bank on how to activate your card. For most banks, the PIN can be activated by simply checking your balance at an ATM.

These cards can be used at PoS (Point of Sale) machines, ATMs, microATMs, to load money into e-wallets, or for online transactions.

Annual charges for credit and debit cards differ from one bank to another, one needs to find out the charges from one's own bank.

2.   USSD (Unstructured Supplementary Service Data

*99# is a USSD (Unstructured Supplementary Service Data) based mobile banking service, by NPCI. To use the service, a customer has to dial *99# from his/her mobile registered with the bank. This feature works on feature phones as well as smart phones, it works on GSM handsets but does not work on CDMA handsets. It does not require an internet connection. There is no need to install any application on a mobile handset to use the service and there are no separate roaming charges for using this service.

The requirements are a bank account, mobile number linked with the bank account (something that can be done online or at an ATM) and to register for USSD or mobile banking (note this step is not the same as linking your mobile number with your bank account). Your bank's ATM has this option. Thereafter, one has to get MMID(mobile money identifier) and get an MPIN(mobile PIN) from one's bank.

Above steps differ from one bank to the other, so you need to contact your bank to know how to register for this service or search online by typing 'how to register for mobile banking+ (name of your bank)', into the search engine.

For the transaction cost, you will have to contact your Telecom Service Provider to know the exact charges for using the service. However, TRAI

To use *99# you have to register your mobile number with your bank

(Telecom Regulatory Authority of India) has set a maximum ceiling of Rs. 0.50 per transaction for using this service.

It is possible to send money to someone who has not registered for mobile banking by using their bank IFSC (Indian Financial System Code) plus account number or with the Adhaar number if the person has linked their Adhaar number with their bank account. IFSC Code is assigned by RBI. This code contains 11 characters and can be found written on the cheque book or on the first page of your pass book.

Funds Transfer limit is Rs 5,000/day per customer and Rs 50,000/annum.

3.   AEPS (Aadhar Enabled Payment System)

The requirement for using this mode of payment is a bank account with Adhaar number linked to that bank account.

Aadhaar Pay is a new Android application for merchants developed jointly by IDFC Bank, NPCI (National Payments Corporation of India) and UIDAI (Unique Identification Authority of India).

Merchants, with a smartphone, have to first install the Aadhar payment app, then create a registered ID. They need a biometric scanner attached to their smart phone, and good internet connectivity, to be able to receive payments.

The customer has to keep their Aadhaar number handy, to make a transaction, they will tell the merchant their Aadhaar number and he will key it into the Aadhar app. The customer will be asked for the name of the bank at which his/her account is linked to the Aadhaar number.

The next step is the customer places their finger at the Aadhar biometric reader. This biometric device is connected to the smart phone that has the Aadhar payment app installed.

Once authenticated, the amount to be paid will be deducted from the customer's bank account and they will receive an SMS from their bank. The customer needs to make sure that they read the SMS to verify that the correct amount has been deducted from their account.

To use AEPS, your Aadhar number must be linked to your bank account

For the system to work, the merchant needs an internet connectivity. The customer does not require internet connectivity. It is not essential to have a phone for this mode of payment however, it helps to carry a phone (either feature or smart), just make sure that mobile number is linked to your bank account. This allows you to check from the SMS received, that the correct amount has been transacted.

There are no transaction costs for this mode of payment and the fund transfer limit is set by individual banks, hence you need to check with your bank.

4. UPI

United Payment Interface (UPI) allows people to send and receive money from one bank account to another. This payment system works on smart phones and requires internet connectivity. The beneficiary must have a VPA (Virtual Payment Address) to be able to receive money.

One prominent example of an app that uses the UPI platform, is BHIM (Bharat Interface for Money). It is an initiative of NPCI to enable cashless payments. Each Bank provides its own UPI App for Android, Windows and iOS mobile platform(s). You could either use your bank's UPI or download and use the BHIM app. Just make sure you download the genuine app from the official Google play store. Do not use any third-party app. Check who is the developer of the app, if it is NPCI then download it, else don't. You certainly don't want to end up downloading a malicious app onto your phone.

To use this mode of payment, all you need is the VPA of the receiver. VPA is a Virtual Payment Address, it is a financial address, it replaces the bank account details and hence it is much simpler to remember and use.

Now, to use this mode of payment you require a bank account, link your mobile number with your bank account, get a smart phone and make sure it is connected to the internet when you use the app. One also needs to keep debit card details handy

Avoid keeping large sums of money in your mobile wallet

for resetting the UPIN for the first time. The UPIN is different from the login passcode that one sees at the opening screen.

Transaction cost is nil, but data charges will depend on the internet services that the user will incur.

The fund transfer limit is 1 lakh / transaction

(Note that this UPIN is different from the MPIN that is used in *99# service).

5. Mobile Wallets

It is an application that can be downloaded onto a smartphone. A mobile wallet is also known as a digital wallet or an e-wallet, it allows one to send and receive payments through it. One can load money into the wallet either through one's bank account or credit/debit card. Main services available through this mode of payment are to check balance in the wallet, to know the history of transactions, and to accept and pay money.

Most banks have their own e-wallets, some popular wallets owned by private companies are Paytm, Freecharge, Mobikwik, Oxigen etc. Funds Transfer limits for users with no KYC (Know your customer) is Rs. 20,000/ month, and for users with full KYC is Rs.1,00,000/- month. For Merchants this limit is Rs. 50,000/ month, and with KYC it is Rs.1,00,000/- month

You need to check with your digital wallet if there are any charges for remittances to bank accounts. This could vary between 0.5% to 2.5%.

6. Internet Banking

Internet Banking is also known as online banking. It allows you to access some banking services, without having to physically visit the bank. It lets you view your accounts, create fixed and recurring deposits and review current deposits, pay utility bills, transfer funds, send requests for new cheque book etc. However, to know the complete list of services available you need to check your own bank's website.

To be able to use this mode of payment you require a bank account, you need to link your mobile

At a micro ATM one can withdraw cash as well as deposit cash

number with bank account and register for Internet Banking.

One can use internet banking through a computer or a smart phone that is connected to the internet. One needs to make sure that the device that is used for payment purposes is free of malware and also has an updated antivirus installed on it.

7. Micro ATMs

A microATM brings the bank to people, it brings banking services to people living in remote areas. Various services can be availed at an MicroATM. A customer can use it through an Aadhar bio-metric authentication system or with a debit-card. It provides a wide range of services to the customers, it can be used for account opening, withdrawing and depositing cash into a bank account, to pay utility bills, to avail services like re-charge of mobiles or DTH connections, for balance enquiry regarding Direct Benefit Transfers of government, in addition, it provides all services available at a regular ATM.

Chapter 11. Laws that Protect Against Online Harassment

How Common is Online Abuse?

According to research, four out of 10 people have been insulted, shamed, stalked, bullied or harassed online. [8]

As per another survey [9] wherein respondents were asked what form of online harassment had they seen, said they had witnessed the following occur to others online:

- 60% of internet users said they had witnessed someone being called offensive names
- 53% had seen efforts to purposefully embarrass someone
- 25% had seen someone being physically threatened
- 24% witnessed someone being harassed for a sustained period of time
- 19% said they witnessed someone being sexually harassed
- 18% said they had seen someone being stalked.

Cybercrime by Motives, in India

	Crime Head	Cyber Crimes By Motives
1.	Revenge /Settling scores	107
2.	Greed/ Money	805
3.	Extortion	73
4.	Cause Disrepute	137
5.	Prank/ Satisfaction of Gaining Control	37
6.	Fraud/ Illegal Gain	1216
7.	Eve teasing/ Harassment	1091
8.	Others	2042
9.	Total	5508

---

[8] (http://www.pewinternet.org/2014/10/22/online-harassment/).

[9] Pew Research Survey of October, 2014

The following table shows the cybercrime by motives, for India, in 2013. Figures are in numbers. (Source: Crime in India 2013, National Crime Records Bureau (NCRB).)

Majority of the cyber offences are economic offences with financial frauds being rampant. One can see from the table, that there are 1216 cases in this category, or roughly 22% of cybercrime cases pertain to fraud and illegal gain. The number of such cases is steadily rising and as per a news report, of November 2015, Norton, a security firm[10] "estimated that 113 million Indians lost about Rs. 16,558 on an average to cybercrime in addition to the "emotional" stress caused by personal financial data breach."

You can see from the above table, that the incidence of online harassment is also quite high. Out of 5508 reported cases of cybercrime, 1091 pertain to online harassment. This means close to 20%, or every fifth case of cybercrime has to do with online harassment.

Knowledge of Laws Can Protect One Against Online Abuse

Public knowledge of laws that are applicable in the online space, equips one to fight against this form of harassment. Awareness might also act as a deterrent for those who feel tempted to indulge in anti-social activities in the digital space.

Here we have mentioned the laws that apply to the internet space, and also how to lodge a complaint with the cyber police.

Some of the laws detailed below are

- IT Amendment Act 2008,
- Some new sections of the Criminal Law (Amendment) Act, 2013. These sections were introduced post-Nirbhaya rape case and are as per the recommendations of the

The Information Technology Act, 2000 is the primary law in India dealing with cybercrime and electronic commerce.

Anyone who uses the internet needs to know that laws regulating the internet exist.

[10] http://www.ndtv.com/india-news/113-million-indians-lost-rs-16-000-on-average-to-cyber-crime-norton-1245142

Justice Verma committee. These laws are women-centric and protect them against online harassment.

- Some sections of the POCSO Act that protect children (those aged below 18 years) against various forms of online harassment and pornography.

Section/ Offence	Description	Punishment
354 A of IPCSexual Harassment	354A. (I) A man committing any of the following acts— (i) physical contact and advances involving unwelcome and explicit sexual overtures; or (ii) a demand or request for sexual favours; or (iii) showing pornography against the will of a woman; or (iv) making sexually coloured remarks, shall be guilty of the offence of sexual harassment.	Any man who commits the offence specified in clause (i) or clause (ii) or clause (iii) of sub-section (1) shall be punished with rigorous imprisonment for a term which may extend to three years, or with fine, or with both.Any man who commits the offence specified in clause (iv) of sub-section (1) shall be punished with imprisonment of either description for a term which may extend to one year, or with fine, or with both.
354C of IPC Voyeurism	Whoever watches a woman engaging in a private act in circumstances where she would usually have the expectation of not being observed either by the perpetrator, or by any other person at the behest of the perpetrator **Explanation 1:** 'Private act', in the context of this provision, is an act carried out in a place which, in the circumstances, would reasonably be expected to provide privacy, and where the victim's genitals, buttocks or breasts are exposed or covered only in underwear; or the victim is	Punishment on first conviction with imprisonment of either description for a term which shall not be less than one year, but may extend to three years, and with fine, and be punished on a second or subsequent conviction, with imprisonment of either description for a term which shall not be less than three years, but may extend to seven years, and also

	using a lavatory; or the person is doing a sexual act that is not of a kind ordinarily done in public. **Explanation 2:** If the victim consented to capture of the images or other material, but not to their dissemination to third persons, such dissemination shall be considered an offence within this section.	with fine.
354D of IPC Stalking	Stalking(1) Any man who— follows a woman and contacts, or attempts to contact such woman to foster personal interaction repeatedly despite a clear indication of disinterest by such woman; or monitors the use by a woman of the internet, email or any other form of electronic communication, commits the offence of stalking; Provided that such conduct shall not amount to stalking if the man who pursued it proves that— it was pursued for the purpose of preventing or detecting crime and the man accused of stalking had been entrusted with the responsibility of prevention and detection of crime by the State; or it was pursued under any law or to comply with any condition or requirement imposed by any person under any law; in the particular circumstances such conduct was reasonable and justified.	(2) Whoever commits the offence of stalking shall be punished on first conviction with imprisonment of either description for a term which may extend to three years, and shall also be liable to fine; and be punished on a second or subsequent conviction, with imprisonment of either description for a term which may extend to five years, and shall also be liable to fine.
509 of IPC	Whoever, intending to insult the modesty of any woman, utters any word, makes any sound or gesture, or exhibits any object, intending that such word or sound shall be heard, or that such gesture or object shall be seen, by such woman, or intrudes upon the privacy of such woman.	Imprisonment for a term which may extend to **one year, or with fine**, or with both.
66B of IT **Act 2008** Dishonestly	Whoever dishonestly receives or retains any stolen computer resource or communication device knowing or	Imprisonment for a term that may extend to 3 years or with fine which

receiving stolen computer resource or communi- cation device	having reason to believe the same to be a stolen computer resource or communication device,	may extend to rupees one lakh or with both.
66C of IT Act 2008 Identity Theft	Whoever, fraudulently or dishonestly make use of the electronic signature, password or any other unique identification feature of any other person	Imprisonment of either description for a term which may extend to three years and shall also be liable to fine which may extend to rupees one lakh.
66D of IT Act 2008 Personation by using computer resources	Whoever, by means of any communi- cation device or computer resource cheats by personation,	Imprisonment of either description for a term which may extend to 3 years and shall also be liable to fine which may extend to one lakh rupees.
66E of IT Act 2008 Violation of Privacy	Whoever, intentionally or knowingly captures, publishes or transmits the image of a private area of any person without his or her consent, under circumstances violating the privacy of that person, shall be punished with imprisonment which may extend to three years or with fine not exceeding two lakh rupees, or with both.Explanation— For the purposes of this section— (a) "transmit" means to electronically send a visual image with the intent that it be viewed by a person or persons; (b) "capture", with respect to an image, means to videotape, photograph, film or record by any means;(c) "private area" means the naked or undergarment clad genitals, pubic area, buttocks or female breast; (d) "publishes" means reproduction in the printed or electronic form	Imprisonment which may extend to three years or with fine not exceeding two lakh rupees, or with both.

	and making it available for public; (e) "under circumstances violating privacy' means circumstances in which a person can have a reasonable expectation that— (f) he or 'he could disrobe in privacy, without being concerned that an image of his private area was being captured; or (g) any part of his or her private area would not be visible to the public, regardless of whether that person is in a public or private place.	
66F of IT Act 2008 Cyber-terrorism	(I) Whoever, — (A) with intent to threaten the unity, integrity, security or sovereignty of India or to strike terror in the people or any section of the people by— (i) denying or cause the denial of access to any person authorised to access computer resource; or (ii) attempting to penetrate or access a computer resource without authorisation or exceeding authorised access; or (iii) introducing or causing to introduce any computer contaminant,and by means of such conduct causes or is likely to cause death or injuries to persons or damage to or destruction of property or disrupts or knowing that it is likely to cause damage or disruption of supplies or services essential to the life of the community or adversely affect the critical information infrastructure specified under section 70; or (B) knowingly or intentionally	Whoever commits or conspires to commit cyber terrorism shall be punishable with imprisonment which may extend to imprisonment for life.

	penetrates or accesses a computer resource without authorisation or exceeding authorised access, and by means of such conduct obtains access to information, data or computer database that is restricted for reasons of the security of the State or foreign relations; or any restricted information, data or computer database, with reasons to believe that such information, data or computer database so obtained may be used to cause or likely to cause injury to the interests of the sovereignty and integrity of India, the security of the State, friendly relations with foreign States, public order, decency or morality, or in relation to contempt of court, defamation or incitement to an offence, or to the advantage of any foreign nation, group of individuals or otherwise, commits the offence of cyber terrorism.	
67 of IT Act 2008 Publishing or transmitting obscene material in electronic form	67. Whoever publishes or transmits or causes to be published or transmitted in the electronic form, any material which is lascivious or appeals to the prurient interest or if its effect is such as to tend to deprave and corrupt persons who are likely, having regard to all relevant circumstances, to read, see or hear the matter contained or embodied in it, shall be punished.	on first conviction with imprisonment of either description for a term which may extend to three years and with fine which may extend to five lakh rupees and in the event of second or subsequent conviction with imprisonment of either description for a term which may extend to five years and also with fine which may extend to ten lakh rupees.

67A of IT Act 2008 Punishment for publishing or transmitting of material containing the sexually explicit act etc., in electronic form	67A Whoever publishes or transmits or causes to be published or transmitted in the electronic form any material which contains sexually explicit act or conduct shall be punished.	on first conviction with imprisonment of either description for a term which may extend to five years and with fine which may extend to ten lakh rupees and in the event of second or subsequent conviction with imprisonment of either description for a term which may extend to seven years and also with fine which may extend to ten lakh rupees.
67B of IT act 2008 Punishment for publishing or transmitting of material depicting children in sexually explicit act etc., in electronic form	67B. Whoever,— (a) publishes or transmits or causes to be published or transmitted material in any electronic form which depicts children engaged in sexually explicit act or conduct; or (b) creates text or digital images, collects, seeks, browses, downloads, advertises, promotes, exchanges or distributes material in any electronic form depicting children in obscene or indecent or sexually explicit manner; or (c) cultivates, entices or induces children to online relationship with one or more children for and on sexually explicit act or in a manner that may offend a reasonable adult on the computer resource; or Punishment for publishing or transmitting of material depicting children in sexually explicit act, etc., In electronic form. (d) facilitates abusing children online; or	shall be punished on first conviction with imprisonment of either description for a term which may extend to five years and with fine which may extend to ten lakh rupees and in the event of second or subsequent conviction with imprisonment of either description for a term which may extend to seven years and also with fine may extend to ten lakh rupees.

	(e) records in any electronic form own abuse or that of others pertaining to sexually explicit act with children, **Explanation.**— *For the purposes of this section, "children" means a person who has not completed the age of 18 years.*Provided that provisions of section 67, section 67A and this section does not extend to any book, pamphlet, paper, writing, drawing, painting representation or figure in electronic form— (i) the publication of which is proved to be justified as being for the public good on the ground that such book, pamphlet, paper, writing, drawing, painting representation or figure is in the interest of science, literature, art or learning or other objects of general concern; or (ii) which is kept or used for bona fide heritage or religious purposes.	
11 of POCSO Act Sexual Harassment	A person is said to commit sexual harassment upon a child when such person with sexual intent, - (i) utters any word or makes any sound, or makes any gesture or exhibits any object or part of body with the intention that such word or sound shall be heard, or such gesture or object or part of body shall be seen by the child; or (ii) makes a child exhibit his body or any part of his body so as it is seen by such person or any other person; or (iii) shows any object to a child in any form or media for pornographic purposes; or	Whoever, commits sexual harassment upon a child shall be punished with imprisonment of either description for a term which may extend to three years and shall also be liable to fine.

	(iv) repeatedly or constantly follows or watches or contacts a child either directly or through electronic, digital or any other means; or (v) threatens to use, in any form of media, a real or fabricated depiction through electronic, film or digital or any other mode, of any part of the body of the child or the involvement of the child in a sexual act; or (vi) entices a child for pornographic purposes or gives gratification there for. **Explanation** – Any question which involves "sexual intent" shall be a question of fact.	
13 of POCSO Act Use of child for pornographic purposes	Whoever, uses a child in any form of media (including programme or advertisement telecast by television channels or internet or any other electronic form or printed form. whether or not such programme or advertisement is intended for personal use or for distribution), for the purposes of sexual gratification, which includes – (a) representation of the sexual organs of a child; (b) usage of a child engaged in real or simulated sexual acts (with or without penetration); (c) the indecent or obscene representation of a child,shall he guilty of the offence of using a child for pornographic purposes. **Explanation:** For the purposes of this section, the expression "use a child" shall include involving a child through any medium like print, electronic, computer or any other technology for preparation,	(1) Whoever, uses a child or children for pornographic purposes shall be punished with imprisonment of either description which may extend to five years and shall also be liable to fine and in the event of second or subsequent conviction with imprisonment of either description tor a term which may extend to seven years and also be liable to fine. (2) If the person using the child for pornographic purposes commits an offence referred to in section 3, by directly participating in pornographic acts, he shall be punished with imprisonment of either description for a term

	production, offering, transmitting, publishing, facilitation and distribution of the pornographic material.	which shall not be less than ten years but which may extend to imprisonment for life, and shall also be liable to fine. (3) If the person using the child for pornographic purposes commits an offence referred to in section 5, by directly participating in pornographic acts, he shall be punished with rigorous imprisonment for life and shall also be liable to fine. (4) If the person using the child for pornographic purposes commits an offence referred to in section 7, by directly participating in pornographic acts, he shall be punished with imprisonment of either description for a term which shall not be less than six years but which may extend to eight years, and shall also be liable to fine. (5) If the person using the child for pornographic purposes commits an offence referred to in section 9, by directly participating in pornographic acts, he shall be punished with imprisonment of either description for a term which shall not be less than eight years but

		which may extend to ten years, and shall also be liable to fine.
15 of POCSO Act Storage of pornographic material involving child	Any person, who stores, for commercial purposes any porno-graphic material in any form involving a child shall be punished.	Imprisonment of either description which may extend to three years or with fine or with both.

How to Lodge a Complaint with the Cyber Police?

If police intervention is necessary, you may find the following tips useful:

- Ensure that offensive, criminal content has been saved up for evidence in the form of a Print screen. Click on the title bar of the window that you want to capture. Press "Alt + PrtScn". A screenshot of your currently active window will be copied to the clipboard. Paste it into your favorite image editor or document editor.

- Please note that Cyber Police will accept a complaint only when it is made in writing.

- To lodge a complaint, please visit the office of the Police in person and file your complaint.

   The information given below, from the Mumbai Cyber Cell website, is useful to understand what information must be provided to file a complaint with the cyber police. Click at the following link for further details:

   http://cybercellmumbai.gov.in/html/faq/information-required-for-complaint.html

If You are a Victim of Hacking

Take the following information with you to lodge a complaint

- Server Logs

Make sure you do not delete any abusive messages, you will need them as evidence when you lodge a complaint with the cyberpolice.

- Copy of defaced web page in soft copy as well as hard copy format, if your website is defaced
- If data is compromised on your server or computer or any other network equipment, soft copy of original data and soft copy of compromised data.
- Access control mechanism details i.e.- who had what kind of the access to the compromised system
- List of suspects – if the victim is suspicious of anyone.
- All relevant information leading to answers of the following questions–
- what ? (what is compromised)
- who? (who might have compromised system)
- when?(when the system was compromised)
- why?(why the system might have been compromised)
- where?(where is the impact of attack-identifying the target system from the network)
- How many?(How many systems have been compromised by the attack)

If You are a Victim of E-mail Abuse, Vulgar E-mail etc.

The police will ask you to submit the following information

- Extract the extended headers of offending e-mail (To find out how to extract header, please refer to the following link. It describes the process for different email accounts. http://cybercellmumbai.gov.in/html/faq/email-headers.html)
- Bring soft copy as well hard copy of offending e-mail.
- Please do not delete the offending e-mail from your e-mail box.
- Please save the copy of offending e-mail on your computer's hard drive.

Teaching Activity

Activity 1: Inform of the Existence of POCSO and IT Act

Objective: Create awareness that there are laws that protect children when they are online.

Material required: None

Steps:

1. Ask students if there are rules that govern the online space, most of them might say 'no'.
2. A small fraction of students would probably be aware of the existence of the IT Act.
3. Explain to them that actions like creating a fake profile, gaining unauthorized access to someone else's account and then using it, are all punishable under the IT Act.

Tell them of the existence of POCSO and the IT Act, 2000 (Information Technology Act, 2000) and IT (Amendment) Act, 2008.

Pocso is an acronym for 'Protection of Children against Sexual Offences Act'. It is applicable to those aged below 18 years of age.

Activity 2- To make a double-sided mask

Objective: To explain why one must not share feelings with people whom you do not know in real life

Materials required

To make an Eye Mask.

2 card sheets of different colors, say blue and red, a pair of scissors, ribbon or elastic for the band, Gum/stapler to fix the band on the mask.

Instructions

Glue together the two card sheets so that each side is a different color. Then draw the pattern, given below, on the card sheet. Cut out the mask. Cut out the holes for the eyes.

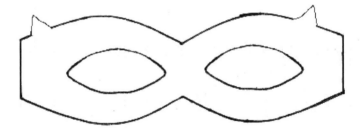

Draw a nice friendly expression on one side and a wicked expression on the other side. Use your imagination to draw these expressions.

Steps:

1. One half of the children will wear the mask with the friendly side up and the other half will not be wearing masks.

2. The children who are not wearing masks will talk to a person wearing the friendly mask. Ask them to talk about themselves. How are they feeling? Why are they upset or angry or disappointed? The friendly mask responds and says some comforting words.

3. Then ask the children wearing masks to reverse the mask and wear it. Now ask them if they still want to share their feelings/emotions with that same person.

4. Next explain to the children that people are anonymous on the internet and there is no way in which one can guess the true identity/intentions of the person.

5. So, one must avoid sharing feelings and other personal details with people whom they have *first* meet on the internet.

Discussion Starters for Parents

1. Discuss with your child the names of a few trusted adults, people whom they can trust and report to in case they experience any uncomfortable situations when they are online.

   Suggest a couple of options so that they know whom to approach in case you are not available. Tell them that the real-world knowledge of grown-ups often helps them provide solutions to problems that youngsters might be facing online.

2. Tell children of the existence of the same good/bad people in the internet world, as in the real world.

3. Share some personal experience to explain to them why it is important for them to inform their trusted adults if anything uncomfortable happens.

Chapter 12. Online Plagiarism

Let's look at the following situation:

Mrs. Mini and Mr. Khorbode are online, searching for information. Mrs. Mini needs it for a presentation that she has to make to her students. Mr. Khorbode is writing a book and he needs some matter for it, and oh, by the way, he is finally completing his long pending book.

They both are happy to have found a lot of relevant information on the net. They soon get busy copying and pasting it, rephrasing it in places, carefully noting down the source of all the information that they are picking out.

As Mr. Khorbode works his way through the vast maze of information, he begins to wonder, "Is all this information on the internet free", "Do I need to take permission from the author of this article?", "How do I contact the author?", he is also wondering," Might be a long time before I get a response from the author".

Mrs. Mini's vs Mr. Khorbode's Use of the Content

Let's begin by answering a question, "Do you think Mrs. Mini or Mr. Khorbode need to take permission when using content from the internet?" And the possible answers are:

1. both of them should take permission
2. only Mr. Khorbode needs to take permission.
3. neither of them need to take permission, everything on the internet is free.

Plagiarizing is taking someone's words or ideas and presenting them as your own

I think option 2, Mr.Khorobde should take permission is the best option. If you think some other option would be good in this situation, do write to us and tell us why you made that choice.

Let us look at the above situation a little more in

detail to understand why we thought option 2 was the best choice.

Mrs. Mini's use of the content is non-commercial, she will use it for a presentation made to her class, and

- she will not be charging her students a fee to view the presentation.
- Her use of the content is only for educational purpose so she can use it without asking for permission.
- But she still needs to document its origin which means she has to cite the source of the information. If she fails to do so, she could be accused of plagiarism.

Next, let us look at Mr.Khorbode's use of the content. He is hoping to sell hundreds of copies of his book and make money out of it. He certainly needs to write in to the website stating how he plans to use their content.

And he also has to be prepared that the author of the content might refuse its use or might demand a fee, particularly when the purpose is commercial.

Our Experience in a Similar Situation

Some time back, we at JaagoTeens, found some useful content and were not sure if we could use it for our Internet Safety workshops in schools. We wrote to the website, and asked them for permission to use their content. They wrote back to us, saying:

'*Will you be conducting presentations in schools for a fee? You are welcome to use the presentations if you provide these workshops free of charge. Since the materials are copyrighted, you also cannot make any changes to the presentations.*'

As you can see they wanted us to use the content for non-commercial purpose only, and secondly, they did not want us to plagiarize the content, which means they asked us not to change the content, and to present it in its original form with all copyright marks in place.

We used their content respecting their terms of use, until we developed our own content.

And then What Happened?

We had worked really hard to get our content ready spending a lot of time, money and resources on it. But then someone used our content ideas to publish a book. We were extremely peeved and saddened to see this happen and it made us realize how important it is to ask the owner of the content permission to use their work.

What did We Learn from this Experience?

It is definitely not a good idea to copy and use someone else's content, without taking their permission. Plagiarism is akin to stealing someone's work, and it can be very disappointing for the author of the work. Besides, one is violating the rights of the owner of that content, so before one uses any content one must take permission from the owner and let them know clearly the intended use of the content.

How to Check for Plagiarism

Children need to learn in school that plagiarism destroys their originality and ability to think creatively

As per the Oxford dictionary, the meaning of plagiarism is the practice of taking someone else's work or ideas and passing them off as one's own.

There are several websites where you can check if some content has been copied from elsewhere. If you type 'plagiarism online free checker 'into a search engine, the search results will throw up a couple of websites that provide this service. They generally ask you to copy and paste a paragraph into a box and then tell you if the content is unique or it has been plagiarized.

Why school and college students need to know that 'cut and paste' is not a great idea

- Students find it easy to copy but this copying kills their originality and ability to think creatively.

- Plagiarism stunts their thinking so it is important to inculcate the healthy habit of reading up good sources, then rewriting relevant information in one's own words.

- Children need to know that even if the information is being rewritten in their own words they still need to cite the source.

We've often asked our college volunteers, and most of them study in reputed colleges, if they know what 'plagiarism' is. Majority of them say that they have not heard of this term, but when we ask if they have ever copied and pasted information from the internet, they invariably say 'yes, everyone does it.'

A common excuse that most college students give is that, "this is something that we have always done ever since we were in school." As this habit starts in school and continues into college, the best time to ask students not to plagiarize is when they are still in school.

Recently, during a discussion on how do college authorities prevent plagiarism, one college volunteer

Children need to learn in school that plagiarism destroys their originality and ability to think creatively

said that their teachers ask them to submit hand-written reports. This does not allow them to simply copy blocks of information into their report.

Example for Citing an Online Source

While citing a source one has to clearly mention from where has the information been taken. It has to include the author's name, the date of publication, the title of article, the book or larger document that the article belongs to and the full url of the page, and not just the home page of the website.

Let's say you wish to cite 20 glossary entries from the website TutorBreeze.com.

Author's name: Leena Gurg

Date of publication: 2010, I could not find the full date

Title of article: Glossary

It belongs to the section: Activities

Gurg, L. (2010). Glossary. In TutorBreeze.com (Activities). Retrieved from http://www.tutorbreeze .com/mod/glossary/view.php?id=20

You can use websites like EasyBib, CitationMachine.net to help you generate citations online. Type in 'citation generator' into a search box of your search engine and then use any of the websites that are displayed in the search results to generate citations for your purpose.

Once you fill in all the relevant information, these websites automatically generate a citation that can be used to cite a source.

Torrent Downloads

- School and college students widely use torrent downloads, their huge popularity stems from the fact that they can be used to share multiple and/or large files such as music albums, movies, software, digital books etc. However, a lot of times the content that is shared might be copyright material, so one needs to make sure that one is not sharing such files.

- Torrents, by themselves, are not illegal, they are simply a transmission protocol that

One can also input the relevant information and generate citations online makes it easier to download files. But the trouble starts when they are used to distribute pirated material. A quick and easy way to avoid such downloads is to verify by a Google search that whatever you are downloading is legitimate.

- If you must torrent, download from a safe uploader. Some websites appoint moderators who rate uploads and uploaders. Look for trusted sources, they are relatively safer to download.

- The most important things to remember while using torrents are:

    (a) Use safe torrents, this will ensure that you do not end up downloading virus or malware onto your system

    (b) Do not violate copyright laws.

Copyright.gov.in

Copyright, as per the Oxford dictionary is the exclusive and assignable legal right, given to the originator for a fixed number of years, to print, publish, perform, film, or record literary, artistic, or musical material.

Details regarding the copyright law in India can be found at the government website, Copyright.gov.in. It lists out various online services, Acts and Rules, and enforcement procedures.

Copyright.gov.in also has comprehensive information regarding infringement of copyright, penalties and the legal remedies in case of infringement. This can be found in the "Copyright Enforcement Toolkit" in the section titled, "Enforcement of Copyright".

Teaching Activities

Objective: To stress the importance of giving credit to the original creator of any work

Activity 1: But, that is my poem!

Material required: Paper, pencil and extra blank sheet for each participant, notice board, pins to put up the poems

Copyright is a legal right created by the law of a country that grants the creator of an original work exclusive rights for its use and distribution

(a) Let children write a poem. Ask them not to write their name on the sheet.

(b) Ask them to display their poem on a notice board

(c) Next, ask them to choose one poem from the one's displayed on the notice-board, tell them not to choose their own poem.

(d) Now ask them to copy the same poem on to another sheet of paper, and submit it with their own name on it.

(e) Read out the poems and judge the best poem and give that person a prize.

(f) The original creator is sure to shout out, "but that was my poem, I should have got the prize for it!"

Then discuss that copying and pasting other's work and passing it off as your own is plagiarism. Even if you reword it, you still need to mention the source of the original work and give credit to the original creator of that work.

2. Pick any online resource. Help the students identify the following

- author's name,
- the date of publication,
- the title of article,
- the book or larger document that the article belongs to and
- the full url of the page.

Then help them write a citation. Also, teach them how to write the same citation using a free online citation generator.

Chapter 13. Privacy Settings for Various Online Platforms

Sheena (name changed) worked for a reputed multinational company. One day she told her friend that she feels uncomfortable as she gets a feeling that her senior stalks her on Whatsapp. Her friend was concerned, she asked, does he send you unwelcome messages, she said 'no', but yesterday he told me 'how can you work in office, if you were up till 2.10 am, yesterday?'

Sheena was shocked and did not know how to react, she felt this was an infringement on her privacy. She knew he was looking at her 'last seen' on Whatsapp.

She then took help from her friend. How did she deal with the situation? Find the answer in this chapter.

Introduction

Many a times, people tend to ignore privacy settings, but one needs to know that **the onus of online safety lies with the user and one has to take charge of one's own privacy.**

Implications of Terms of Service, privacy settings, etc. can be very confusing for most of us. Services and versions are frequently upgraded and privacy settings that are valid today might not hold good 3 months down the line, so there is a need to constantly monitor the settings of one's account.

There is also an option to watch online videos on safety settings, etc. and then to follow those instructions to configure privacy settings on one's account.

It is also important to understand what one is signing up for and to keep abreast of changes.

Here we have discussed privacy settings on

- Social networking sites- FaceBook, Twitter, LinkedIn, MySpace
- Mobile apps – Whatsapp, Instagram and SnapChat.
- Photosharing sites - Flickr, Pinterest

Facebook

About Facebook

- Facebook is an online social networking service.
- It was founded on February 4, 2004 by Mark Zuckerberg with his college roommates and fellow Harvard University students Eduardo Saverin, Andrew McCollum, Dustin Moskovitz and Chris Hughes.

- The founders had initially limited the website's membership to Harvard students, but later expanded it to colleges in the Boston area, the Ivy League, and Stanford University.

- Facebook now allows anyone who claims to be at least 13 years old to become a registered user of the website.

- According to an article in the Times of India, India has over 125 million Facebook Users, second largest user base in the world, the largest being the US.

Your Information on FaceBook

- It is very important to remember that one's Facebook account slowly turns into a massive storehouse of personal information. Some of this being stored when a user creates his/her profile, example, name, age, e-mail address, etc, while other information keeps getting added along the way, as one posts status updates, photos, videos, messages, chats and a lot more.

- To prevent misuse, it is essential to configure one's Privacy Settings; this keeps the user's information safe and gives him/her control over who can view what information.

- Facebook requires you to disclose some information compulsorily. This includes your name, age, gender, and e-mail address. NOTHING else is compulsory, even if the website prompts you for information (like your mobile no, siblings, workplace, etc.) you can skip filling them in.

- Information such as your Profile Picture, Cover Picture, and networks (Friends/Employers) are available to EVERYONE.

Privacy settings for each platform are different so one needs to spend some time to understand them and then to configure settings for one's account based on one's preferences.

At times, the default privacy settings might change so keep reviewing them periodically and do not assume that that since you have configured them once, the settings will remain valid in future.

[11] (Source: *https://en.wikipedia.org/wiki/Facebook*).

[12] (*http://timesofindia.indiatimes.com/tech/tech-news/Facebooks-user-base-touches-125-million-in-India/articleshow/47866523.cms*

Even the strictest Privacy Settings cannot alter this.

- Instructions for settings up one's privacy settings can also be found at https://www.facebook.com/about/basics/

Privacy Settings on Facebook

To begin configuring your privacy settings, click on the shortcut marked with a red circle, below, you can find it next to the Home button.

Step 1 - Click on the Privacy Settings Shortcut

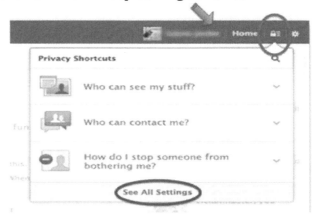

2. Step 2

Step 2 – Change your Privacy Settings according to this example

Step 2

1. Click on the 'Privacy' button in the left side tool bar.
2. Next configure settings for each of the following sections
   - Who can see my stuff?
   - Who can contact me?
   - Who can look me up?

Step 3 – Limit the content that is posted on your Timeline as per this example

1. Click on 'Timeline and Tagging' seen in the left hand column.
2. Configure your settings in each of the following sections
   - Who can add things to my timeline?
   - Who can see things on my timeline?
   - How can I manage tags people add and tagging suggestions?

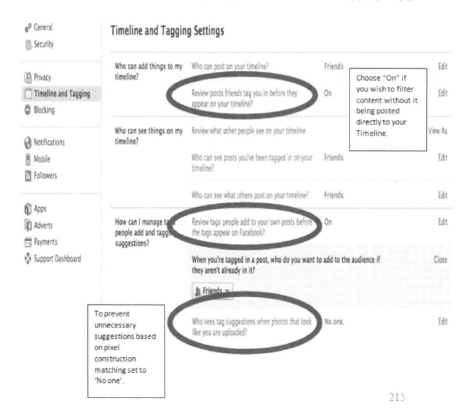

215

Step 4 – Review your Timeline as an outsider

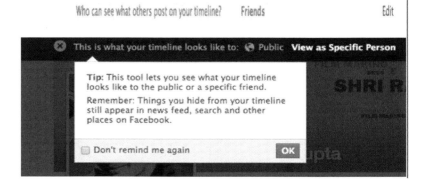

- To reach this page
    - o   click on your name,
    - o   Next, click on the three dots next to "View your activity" button. Here choose "View as".
- this step lets you know how much of your information is publicly visible. You can once again go back and alter your settings if you are not happy with the information visible here. Do not hesitate to alter the option from "Friends" to "Only Me" for certain menus as per your level of comfort.

To further strengthen your privacy settings, you can follow the steps given below.

Other Settings

5.   Friends Lists – Use This to Share Wisely

In real life, you would normally have a very close group of friends, some others who are just acquaintances, relatives (close and distant), colleagues and so on. You can group your online friends into different categories under "Friends" on your Facebook screen. This will help determine what and with whom you will share how much information, e.g. photos, etc.

6. Tagging photos and videos

You have a choice. Go to 'Privacy' – 'Profile' – 'Photos Tagged of You' - Click on "Customize" from drop down menu and choose "Only Me". Repeat for 'Videos Tagged of You'. This will prevent tagged photos from appearing in your friends' 'News Feeds'. Remember to 'Save'. You can always choose from Friends List to selectively share photos.

7. Personal data

Remember, once this appears on the Net, you will have no control over what is picked up and passed on. So, think carefully and determine how much you want to share in the two information pages 'Basic" and 'Contact information' under Privacy-Profile, as these include telephone numbers, address, email ids, birthday, relationship status, etc.

8. Login

To access the legitimate Facebook site, it is safest to just type "Facebook.com" into your browser. Avoid clicking a URL that looks different as it may lead to a phishing site that appears a replica of your Facebook login page. Keep updating your browsers since latest versions of some browsers like Internet Explorer and Safari warn users if they are in a suspected phishing site.

9. Applications

When using third party applications, the element of risk lies in the fact that in order to run the desired application, your personal details need to be accessed by that application. Hence, your privacy might be compromised. We also suggest you take responsibility and check what information an app has access to and then edit its settings to suit you. If you do not wish to keep an app then you can remove it. If you think that an app is abusive then make sure you report it on Facebook.

10. Report Abuse

(a) Don't ignore but make sure you report offensive, abusive or obscene content. Click on "Actions" button next to the post. Use the "Report" link that appears near the

> Even the best privacy settings cannot keep sensitive information secure, so don't post any information that can harm you if it becomes public.

content itself (whether it's a photo, message, post or something else).

(b) If someone creates a fake account and pretends to be you, make sure you report it to FaceBook. Go to the cover photo and click on the row of 3 dots. Choose the "Report" option and then follow the instructions on the screen to complete the process.

11. Put your correct age

'If you are 12 years old don't say you are 21 years old'.

12. Unfriend or block someone

1. To unfriend someone:

   Go to that person's profile

   Place the mouse on 'Friends' that is visible on the cover picture

   Select Unfriend

   The person you unfriended won't be notified. If you unfriend someone, you'll be removed from their friend list.

   You can still view each other's public profile and send each other a friend request at a later point of time, if you wish to be friends again.

2. To block someone:

   Go to that person's profile

   Next to 'Following' and 'Message' you will find three horizontal dots. Click on them.

   Choose Block from the drop- down menu.

   The person you block won't be notified. If you block someone you will be removed from their friend list. You cannot search each other on Facebook and the person cannot send you a friend request unless you unblock him/her.

You'll find more information about how to report things in the FaceBook Help Center:

https://www.facebook.com/help

Instagram

About Instagram

- **Instagram** is an online mobile photo-sharing, video-sharing, and social networking service that enables its users to take pictures and videos, and share them either publicly or privately on the app.

- It also allows sharing through a variety of other social networking platforms, such as Facebook, Twitter, Tumblr, and Flickr.

- Users can apply digital filters to their images, effects that can be used to make a picture look different, maybe brighter, darker, with something written on it etc .

- An Instagram video can be 3 to 60 seconds long.
- Instagram was created by Kevin Systrom and Mike Krieger, and launched in October 2010 as a free mobile app.[13]

As per a Google search, Instagram has close to 300 million users, worldwide.

This app is used to share photos and videos on phones and is more popular with the younger age group. As per the PewInternet.org website about 87% of internet users in 18-29 years age group use Instagram.

http://www.pewinternet.org/2015/01/09/demographics-of-key-social-networking-platforms-2/

Privacy Settings on Instagram

Here we have discussed five simple steps to configure your privacy settings. For more details or specific issues please visit the help center.

1. Set your account to be a Private Account

People can upload photos and videos to Instagram and then share them with a select group of friends. You have an option of keeping your account public or private. By default, an account is public which means anyone can view your profile and posts. If you want to share your posts only with a select crowd of people, then set your account to Private.

Depending on the phone that you own there might be slight difference in the settings.

Windows Phone

1. Go to your profile by tapping [⬛]
2. Tap **Edit Profile**
3. Turn on the **Posts are Private** setting by checking the box and then tap the check mark to save your changes

2. To block someone if you don't want them to access your posts

When you block a person they don't receive a notification so they don't get to know that you have blocked them. Here's how to block or unblock someone:

1. Tap their username to open their profile
2. Tap [⋯] (iPhone/iPad), [⋮] (Android) or ••• (Windows)
3. Tap **Block User**

3. Report abuse- a single post or a profile

If you see a post or profile that is against the Instagram Community Guidelines (ex: nudity, spam, self-harm), you can report it.

---

[13] (Source: https://en.wikipedia.org/wiki/Instagram)

(a) To report a post:

    1. Tap ••• (iOS and Windows Phone) or ⋮ (Android) below the post

    2. Tap **Report Inappropriate**

    3. Follow the on-screen instructions

(b) To report a profile:

    1. Tap ⬆ (iOS), ••• (Windows Phone) or(Android) in the top right of the profile

    2. Tap **Report Inappropriate** (iOS and Android) or **Report for Spam** (Windows Phone)

    3. Follow the on-screen instructions

4. Declining or Accepting messages, sent through Instagram Direct, by someone you don't know

If someone you don't follow sends you a message, it'll appear as a request in your inbox. To decline or allow the message, tap the message then select **Decline** or **Allow** at the bottom of the screen. You can also tap **Ignore All** to ignore all requests at one time. Once you allow a message request from someone, their future messages will go directly to your inbox.

5. Visibility of posts that you share on other social networks like FaceBook, Twitter etc.

Private posts that you share to social networks may be visible to the public depending on your privacy settings for those networks. For example, a post you share to Twitter that was set to private on Instagram may be visible to the people who can see your Twitter posts.

Once you make your posts private, people will have to send you a follow request if they want to see your posts.

Additional Information

- If you can't find the person you want to block or unblock, they may have deleted their account or their profile may be unavailable to you.

- If you don't have an Instagram account, you can report someone using a form that can be found at the following link- https://help.instagram.com. If you're trying to report a post or profile you can't see, ask a friend who can see the content to report it.

- Your profile gives you all your information at a glance, your photos, videos and settings. Here, you can view the pictures you've shared, the people you're following and who's following you. To access the Instagram Help Centre, please use the following url :https://help.instagram.com.

Whatsapp

About Whatsapp

Whatsapp Messenger is a cross-platform mobile messaging app which allows you to exchange messages without having to pay any SMS charges.[14]

According to a report in LiveMint [15]

- 56% of Internet Users in India use WhatsApp every day
- It is the most popular instant messaging app in India
- It has 1.2 billion monthly active users globally in January 2017, with close to 200 million users in India.

With its usage being so prevalent, let us take a look at the safety features that can help one steer clear of any trouble while on this messaging app.

Privacy Settings in Whatsapp in Four Easy Steps

There are slight differences in the sequence that you need to follow, depending on whether you have an Android, Windows or Apple phone. So, please visit the help center of the application and check, if required.

Go to WhatsApp > Menu Button > **Settings** > **Account** >**Privacy**.

1. Last Seen

If you do not wish others to see when are you online, turn this off. You have three choices here

- Everyone: If you choose Everyone then all WhatsApp users can see your 'last seen',
- My Contact: then the app uses names from your phone's address book and they can see if you are online.
- or Nobody: means you are not visible to anyone.

2. Visibility of Profile photo

The next option is your profile photo. It can also be made visible to Everyone, your contacts (all names saved in your phone Address Book) and Nobody

3. Status

The third option is to change your status. This also gives you the same three options, it can be visible to Everyone, your Contacts or Nobody.

4. Blocking

If someone is being abusive or simply because the contact is not a friend, but just an acquaintance or colleague, you might want to block them.

---

[14] (Source: https://www.whatsapp.com/)

[15] http://www.livemint.com/Industry/vU55FbKdlz9vIfkxUb0EoL/Facebook-tops-networking-WhatsApp-in-message-apps-in-India.html

To block a contact on Whatsapp while you keep the number on your phone

Now we answer the question that we asked at the beginning of the chapter.

Sheena followed the above steps to block her senior from her Whatsapp account.

She chose **Options** > **Settings** > **Account** > **Privacy** > Blocked Contacts

Tap 'Add New' and select the number from your phone contacts.

Next check your blocked contact list to verify that the blocked contact appears here.

To block an unknown number, people who are not in your contact list take the following steps

If you have been receiving messages from unknown people, numbers that are not saved in your phone, then follow the following sequence to block the sender:

1.   Open WhatsApp
2.   Open the chat window with the unknown contact.
3.   Go to **Options** > **Block**.

Twitter

About Twitter

Twitter is an online social networking service that enables users to send and read short 140-character messages called "tweets". Registered users can read and post tweets, but unregistered users can only read them.

As per Twitter, it has 320 million active users and 500 million tweets going out in a single day.

Privacy Settings

1.   To share tweets with a select crowd of people.

After setting up a Twitter account.

(a) Click on "Profile and Settings", next to the Tweet button. Choose "Settings", choose "Security and privacy". One of the options under Privacy reads "Protect my Tweets". Note that the default setting is Public, you might want to firstly, set this to private, however an authorized third party application may be able to see your protected tweets.

2.   Public vs Private Tweets

Now if yours is a personal account, and you don't want unknown people looking at your tweets, then select the option "Protect my Tweets". The risk in not selecting this option is that unknown people, even those without a twitter account, could be watching your tweets, they can copy, download and re-share your tweets.

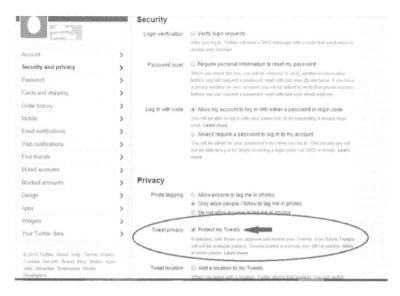

In case you have set up an account for an ngo/group/organization, and you wish to make your tweets publicly available, then you could leave the Protect my Tweets box unchecked. In such a case, you are treating your twitter account as a place to reach out to the public, and not as a platform to exchange personal information with friends/colleagues etc.

3. Tweet Location

Make sure you understand what does the option **"Tweet location"** do, you could choose a location of your choice, or you could choose the precise location that you are tweeting from. Twitter itself cautions you to be careful while using this feature. It says," **Just like you might not want to Tweet your home address, please be cautious when Tweeting from locations that you don't want others to see".**

4. Mute, block or report content on Twitter

You can mute, block or report content on Twitter. The following briefly describes what do each of these options do.

Mute: you might have some contacts who have a lot to tweet, just as in a group of friends you have some people who talk a lot, and at times you need some quiet, you wish they could shut up for some time. In the same way, some friends might be sending out a lot of tweets, but you don't want to keep receiving them. Since you do not plan to remove these friends from your contact list, you can use Mute option to stop getting their tweets on your timeline. Click on their name and you are directed to their profile. Next click on the gear icon and choose Mute from it. They will not get to know that you have muted their tweets.

Block: at times you might not want some contacts to access your account. In that case you can block them; they will not be able to view your profile, or reply to your tweets or mention you or tag you or send you a direct message. Their tweets will also not appear on your timeline.

Report: if you feel that some account is posting harassing or threatening or inappropriate content, then there is an option to report that account to Twitter. We all have a social responsibility towards keeping the internet a pleasant and safe place to be in, and hence do not ignore abusive accounts and let them be. You can report a profile, or an individual tweet or even report on behalf of someone else.

To report a profile

- Click on the profile name
- Once the profile opens click on the gear icon
- Select Report and provide description of why you think the tweet is inappropriate.

To report a Tweet

- Navigate to the Tweet you'd like to report.
- Click or tap the More icon (...
- Select Report.
- If you select 'They're being abusive or harmful', you will be asked to provide additional information about the issue you're reporting.

Think Before You Post

All these social platforms are very public places, and are deceptively quiet, leading you to believe that you are the only one out there, but never believe that, and constantly keep reminding yourself, there are more than a billion eyes who could be reading every single word that you post. Do not vent out your anger, resentment, emotions, private moments on these platforms, damage-control can be an extremely difficult and an emotionally- draining task.

Twitter also cautions you,

- If you have authorized a third-party application to access your account, that third-party application may be able to see your protected Tweets.
- Keep in mind that when you choose to share content on Twitter with others, this content may be downloaded or re-shared.

   (https://support.twitter.com/articles/14016)

   Details on reporting tweets can be read at: https://support.twitter.com/articles/15789

SnapChat

About SnapChat

SnapChat is an image messaging application software. According to Statistisia.com, 10% of India's mobile users have SnapChat on their phones.

The app is popular amongst teenagers, and is widely used to share pictures.

According to comScore.com, 45% of SnapChat users are in the 18-24 years old, however it is believed that these figures might not be exact since their survey does not account for users who are below 18 years of age.

Its unique feature is that the shared picture appears for a few seconds and then disappears. However, this feature needs to be clearly understood as minors end up sharing pictures that are illegal or sexual in nature, mostly assuming that the pics uploaded don't run the risk of becoming public.

15 s and the pic is gone, but it can still be saved

The assumption that pictures on SnapChat cannot be saved is not true. It is possible to store any image that is shared on this platform. This can be done in the following ways:

- Anyone can take a screenshot of a Snap(photo or video)
- Another camera can be used to save a picture of a Snap that appears on one screen

Effects like doodles and stickers can be removed from snaps

There are ways of doing it. Let us say, someone clicks a nude selfie and then covers up some parts of the image with doodles and stickers. The sender needs to know that these effects can be removed from a snap; and it is best to avoid sending these images that you know can only lead to embarrassment and legal trouble.

The above is from SnapChat's support page and is given under Safety Tips and Resources. This information can be viewed at the following url: https://support.snapchat.com/en-US/a/safety-tips-resources

Practical Tips While Using the Platform

Here are a few more safety precautions that one needs to follow, these are common to most other social media applications, also.

- **Behave towards others in a way in which you would like them to behave with you. Do not be rude**!
- Check your privacy settings. Make sure you understand them.
- Keep a strong password.
- In case of harassment, block a person and report them to the website.
- Talk to a trusted adult if there is anything that makes you uncomfortable.

LinkedIn

About LinkedIn

LinkedIn is a business-oriented social networking service. Founded in December 14, 2002 and launched on May 5, 2003, it is mainly used for professional networking. As of October 2015, LinkedIn reported more than 400 million acquired users in more than 200 countries and territories.[16]

Privacy Settings

In 5 simple steps see how can you make sure that you have control over what information you are sharing.

When you move your cursor over your profile photo at the top right corner of your homepage, you see a drop-down menu. From this menu, select 'Privacy and Settings.' Now you will see 3 different links at the top of the page, Account, Privacy, and Communications.

1. Account

This has 3 categories- Basics, Third-party and Subscriptions.

Basics

- Make sure you have a strong password. Keep a mix of small letters, caps, numbers and special characters. Do not use any dictionary words, or any personal information, not even your cat's name!
- If you add a phone number, then people can use it to find you and try to connect with you. Decide if you wish to keep this feature on or off.
- "Where you're signed in", this options lets you sign out of all active sessions. If you detect some unfamiliar activity here, eg. if it shows that you have signed in from some place and you know that you were not at that location, then make sure you change your password. This could mean that someone who knows your password has accessed your account.

Third Parties

Here you can see a list of apps that have access to your profile. If you find any apps that you do not like, select them and then choose remove them.

Subscription and Closing the account

- Here one can view any subscription-based offers
- You have the option of closing your LinkedIn account.

2. Privacy

Here you can configure the following settings- your profile privacy, blocking and hiding, data privacy and advertising and security. Go through each of these links to see what information is publicly visible and modify settings according to your own preferences.

Profile privacy

- Edit your public profile, this shows how your profile appears in search engines. Click here and edit whatever you do not wish to be publicly visible.

---

[16] (Source: *https://en.wikipedia.org/wiki/LinkedIn*)

- Tells you who can see your connections, you might not want people to see your full list of connections, in which case you can turn this off.

- How you rank, this shows how you compare with your connections in terms of profile views. If you don't want others to see you or your standings in their How You Rank page, then you can turn this feature off. This feature also lets you know how you could improve your page ranking and set it to 'on' or 'off' depending on how useful you think the feature is.

- The button at "Viewers of this profile also viewed", lets you set it to on or off.

- Sharing profile edits, if you change your profile, or make recommendations or follow someone, you have a choice if you want that information to be shared with your connections or not. Keep it on or off depending on whether your answer is yes or no, respectively.

- Profile viewing options, you might view others profile but might not want to disclose your own identity. Choose an option that best suits you.

Blocking and Hiding

- If you choose 'everyone' then people who are not your connections can also view your public updates.

- If there are some connections whom you have blocked, then you can change that here. (Go to the profile of the person you'd like to block or report. Move your cursor over to the down arrow next to the button in the top section of the member's profile and select Block or report from the list.)

- Unfollowed follow back those you might have unfollowed.

MySpace

About MySpace

Myspace is a social networking website offering an interactive, user-submitted network of friends, personal profiles, blogs, groups, photos, music, and videos.

It is headquartered in Beverly Hills, California.

It has close to 50 million active users as per the following website. http://expandedramblings.com/index.php/myspace-stats-then-now/

1.   First off, Set your Profile to Private:

Sign-in to your MySpace account. Go to 'Classic View of the profile', click on 'Account Settings' link located next to your profile picture. In 'New Home Skin' view of the profile, click on 'Settings' from Control Panel under your profile picture. Select 'Privacy' from the top navigation bar. In 'Profile Viewable By' select 'My Friends Only'. *Save.*

2. Control visibility of comments:

After going to the 'Settings' feature as described in Item 1 above, select 'Spam' and in 'Comments' choose 'Require approval before comments are posted,' thus avoiding unwanted or embarrassing comments *Save*.

3. Action against unwanted users:

You can block other users if you don't wish to interact with him/her any more. Go to user's page and under their profile picture select 'Block User' link. Click 'Ok.' to confirm in the pop-up window. *Save*.

4. Stay invisible:

Turn off 'Online Now" icon so no one knows when you are online on MySpace. Go to 'Settings' feature as described in Item 1 above, select 'Privacy' and in 'Online now' you have to un-select 'Show People when I'm Online.' *Save*.

MySpace has several built-in security measures such as:

- Age is locked on sign-up for minors.
- 'Teachable moments' offered at edit/upload stage.
- Minors have tools to stop Cyberbullying. They can deny permission to upload comments.
- Verification of email addresses by MySpace;
- Algorithms and tools run 24x7 to identify underage users and delete such profiles;
- It disallows an adult who wants to contact known underage user.
- Adults cannot browse for minors due to a default setting on under-16s.
- They run 'Sentinel Safe' to identify / match known offenders from law enforcement's database.

Privacy on Photo-Sharing websites

*Due to continuous development and upgradation of services by these online platforms, **it is best to periodically review their privacy information** on their websites!*

Remember that any online platform is open to hacking and, therefore, whatever the privacy settings, nothing is foolproof. Use photo-sharing websites only if you are absolutely sure you want to put them online. Here we have discussed settings in Flickr and Pinterest.

Flickr

Flickr is a photo-sharing and hosting service. Here people can share and explore each other's photos.

Privacy settings:

If you wish, you can set your default privacy settings for all your photos on Flickr to 'Private'. One can also choose to select certain photographs to be marked as 'Private' by clicking on 'Edit' next to the photo and choosing the setting 'Only You,' 'Your friends,' 'Your family,' or 'Anyone'.

As for Google, even Flickr gives a user the option of 'Usage License' being granted to Creative Commons. For more details, please view http://www.flickr.com/tour/share/

Pinterest

Pinterest is a social network that allows users to share, and post (known as 'pinning' on Pinterest) images or videos to their own or see what other users have pinned.

To stop search engines like Google and Yahoo! from showing your Pinterest profile:

1. Click your name at the top of Pinterest.
2. Click the gear menu, then settings.
3. Switch Search Privacy from No to Yes.
4. Click Save Settings.

   https://help.pinterest.com/en/articles/edit-your-account-privacy

   Hide your account from search engines

   Hide your Pins from other people

   Disable posting to Facebook or Twitter

   Unfollow Facebook Friends

   Disable cookie-based personalization

JaagoTeens Survey

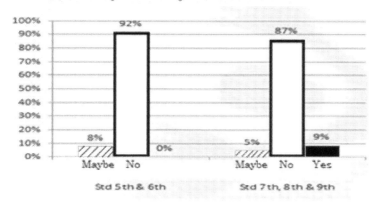

Have you ever uploaded a photo that you would not want your family to know about?

Pictures are no longer stored in the family's Kodak camera film roll, in today's internet world, children are clicking pictures on their own, and then they are the sole decision-makers regarding what to post, therefore it is important to educate them and enable them to take safe decisions about what to post, and what not to post.

Our question to students of 5th, 6th, 7th, 8th and 9th std students was, "Have you ever uploaded a photo that you would not want your family to know about?"

Responses from children were as follows:

Std 5 and 6th: 8 % of the young students had exposed themselves to risk by uploading photographs that they knew their families would not approve of. So, out of a group of 250 students almost 20 students might have uploaded such photographs.

Std 7,8 and 9th: Almost 14% of older children had uploaded personal photos that they would not have shared with their family. Again, out of 250 students as many as 35 students had uploaded such pictures. The desire to experiment and take risky decisions, appears to be higher in the 12-15 years group. This once again emphasizes the need to counsel students and tell them of the trouble that they might get into if their pictures end up with the 'wrong' kind of people.

Suggested Activities for teachers

1. Percentage of teenagers sharing their personal information, online

Objective: To tell youngsters what information is not to be shared online.

Display the following slide. Ask students which of the following items, shown on the slide, have they posted online. Then explain to them that one can carry out one's activities on the internet without making this information public. Discuss with them why displaying this information can be risky.

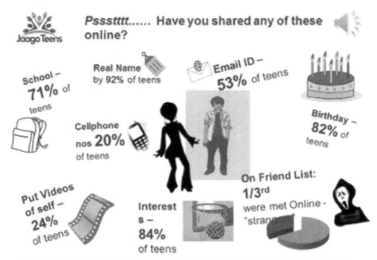

Pssstttt...... Have you shared any of these online?

Real Name by 92% of teens

Email ID – 53% of teens

School – 71% of teens

Cellphone nos 20% of teens

Birthday – 82% of teens

Put Videos of self – 24% of teens

Interests – 84% of teens

On Friend List: 1/3rd were met Online - "strangers"

Source: http://www.pewinternet.org/Infographics/2013/Teens-Social-Media-And-Privacy.aspx dated May 21,2013

Stats in the slide are from the following url. http://www.pewinternet.org/2013/05/21/teens-social-media-and-privacy/

Activity 2. Is it possible to guess how many people might view your profile?

Objective: Understanding that just one or two strangers on your friend list is equivalent to having hundreds of strangers on your friend list.

During workshops students invariably tell us,*'Every stranger is not bad. Why do you say don't talk to strangers?'*

1. Ask children to draw this sketch in their note books. First, they draw a circle to show their own selves and then another 2 lines. Draw two circles at the end of the lines to denote 2 strangers

2. Next from each of these circles, ask them to draw two more lines. Then they can draw 4 circles at the end of the lines to denote 4 strangers.

3. Let them draw another two levels with 8 and 16 circles respectively. Tell them they are drawing heads of strangers, unknown people who might be viewing their profile.

4. Then explain to them how even one stranger on their friend list exposes them to risk and even the strictest of privacy settings does not guarantee them hundred percent against unknown people.

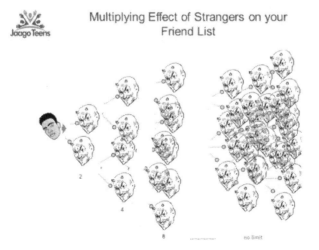

Multiplying Effect of Strangers on your Friend List

Discussion starters for Parents/Trusted Adults

1. Ask children names of a couple of websites they enjoy visiting.
2. Ask them to choose a website where you could work together with them to configure the privacy settings.
3. Once they have chosen a website, spend some time to see how to reach the page that gives a description of the privacy settings. Your child might find it difficult to understand the settings so explain these to him/her.
4. As you configure the privacy settings, tell them why you have made a particular choice. Many a times, it is not very simple to understand the settings, so make sure you are able to spend adequate time configuring the settings to your satisfaction.

College students attending sessions on Safe Internet Usage

Corporates and Teachers attending a training session

Children enjoying games that teach them how to use the Internet safely

Some team members and JaagoTeens puppets

Attending a presentation and writing what they understood by Internet Safety

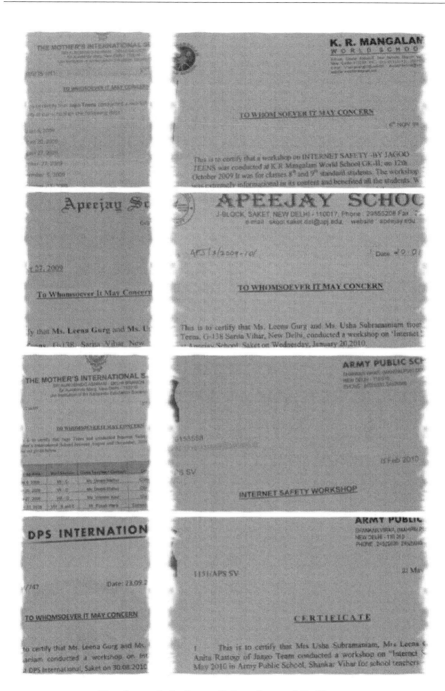

Testimonials from Schools and Colleges

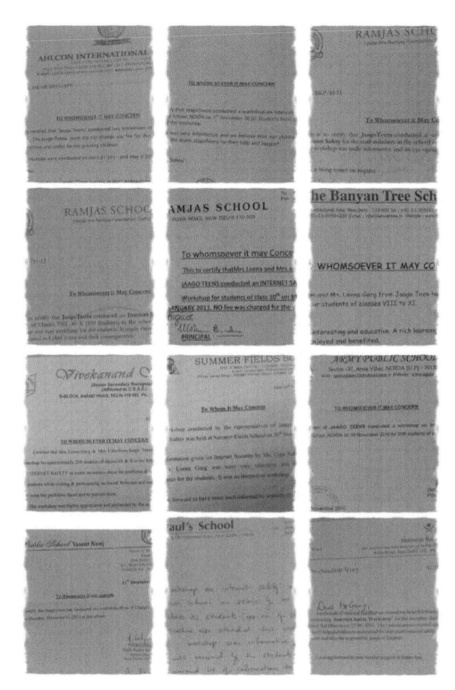

Testimonials from Schools and Colleges

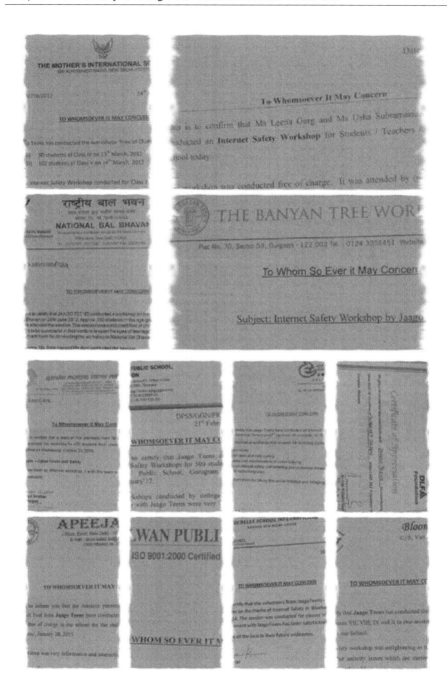

Testimonials from Schools and Colleges

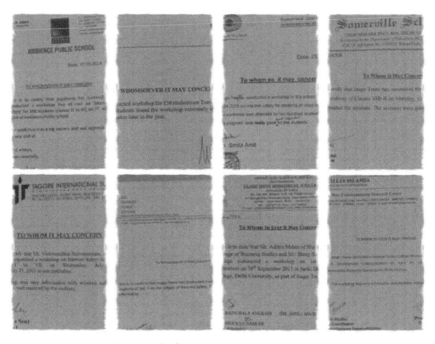

Testimonials from Schools and Colleges

Made in the USA
Middletown, DE
03 October 2021

49532291R00088